Frank Boyden
of Deerfield

Frank Boyden of Deerfield

*The Vision and Politics of
an Educational Idealist*

Brian P. Cooke

MADISON BOOKS
Lanham • New York • Oxford

Copyright © 1994 by Madison Books
First paperback printing 2000

Published by Madison Books
4720 Boston Way
Lanham, Maryland 20706

12 Hid's Copse Road
Cumnor Hill, Oxford OX2 9JJ, England

Distributed by National Book Network

The hardback edition of this book was previously catalogued
by the Library of Congress as follows:

Cooke, Brian.
Frank Boyden of Deerfield : the vision and politics of
an educational idealist / by Brian Cooke.
p. cm.
Includes bibliographical references and index.
1. Deerfield Academy. 2. Boyden, Frank L. (Frank
Learoyd), 1879–1972. 3. School principals— United
States— Biography. I. Title.
LD7501.D363C66 1994
373.744'22— dc20 94–17513 CIP

ISBN 1-56833-033-2 (cloth : alk. paper)
ISBN 1-56833-158-4 (pbk. : alk. paper)

♾™ The paper used in this publication meets the minimum requirements of
American National Standard for Information Sciences— Permanence of
Paper for Printed Library Materials, ANSI/NISO Z39.48-1992.
Manufactured in the United States of America.

For Monica

and

For Mom and Dad

CONTENTS

Contents

PREFACE

Much criticism is directed today at American schools and school leadership. Although education critics and reformers often focus on the structural deficiencies of our school system, they tend to understate the importance of personal leadership. Contemporary principals and headmasters are more burdened than ever by budget cuts, bureaucracy, tort claims, court orders, clerical duties, union demands, and parental expectations. These overwhelming forces demand unprecedented vision, dedication, management, and leadership skills.

Concerned as we are about immediate educational problems and their long term consequences, we may use history to gain perspective on the present and develop prescriptions for the future. This interpretation of Frank L. Boyden, Deerfield Academy headmaster 1902-1968, explores the connection between quality schooling and inspirational school leadership. It is both historical and biographical, a compelling American success story. It is also a case study for leaders not only in education but in all enterprises.

Frank Boyden's tenure as headmaster of Deerfield Academy spanned seven decades. It began in the waning days of horse travel and ended with astronauts standing on the moon. In peacetime and at war, through good times and bad, Frank Boyden insisted the high school was one of few places in an imperfect world where students could approach the ideals of simplicity, goodness, understanding, charity, and mutual respect.

Like all great leaders, Boyden envisioned a worthy ideal, defined a strategic plan to achieve it, and inspired others to join him in the quest. Boyden's most notable associates included United States President Calvin Coolidge, advertising genius Bruce Barton, and Wall Street brokerage giant Charles E. Merrill. Together with other well-connected supporters, these philanthropists financed Boyden's ambitious educational blueprint.

Preface

Although Frank Boyden is most often remembered for building a superior private academy, his influence extends beyond the New England boarding school world. Actively involved in local, state, and national politics, Boyden served as a delegate to the 1917 Massachusetts Constitutional Convention. Theodore Roosevelt's American Playground and Recreation Commission recruited him. Franklin D. Roosevelt appointed him to the National Youth Administration. Harry S Truman requested his service on the Navy Civilian Advisory Commission. Dwight D. Eisenhower celebrated a presidential birthday with a ride in his horse-drawn carriage. John F. Kennedy and Richard M. Nixon honored him with personal invitations to the White House.

Those who consider Frank Boyden a hero and role model are legion. Fifty former students and faculty have led schools of their own. Twelve became college presidents. Many more principals, headmasters, and chief executive officers cite Boyden as a primary influence on their own leadership styles.

Amidst our well-intentioned efforts to identify and correct what is wrong with American schools, we sometimes overlook what is right. Frank Boyden's lifelong contributions to private and public secondary and higher education remind us of the best we have been and will continue to be with sustained earnestness and dedication to a selfless ideal.

Brian Cooke
Albuquerque, New Mexico
5 May 1994

1

"A LITTLE BUG"

Bob Maynard and Frank Boyden sat beneath a shade tree moments after graduating from Amherst College in 1902. Tall and strapping, Maynard was a brilliant, popular student bound for Harvard Law School. Boyden, by contrast, was short and bespectacled. With his hair amply greased and parted in the middle, he was a far less heroic figure.

"This poor little boy with his back against a gum tree," Maynard remembered Boyden. "He looked like a little bug in his cap and gown."

"Well, Bill, what next?" Maynard asked, using Boyden's familiar nickname.

"I don't know," Boyden said. "I always wanted to be a lawyer. But I suppose I'll have to teach until I get enough money for law school."

Uncertain about the future, Boyden returned to his hometown, Foxboro, Massachusetts, where he busied himself organizing potato sack and wheelbarrow races, a tug-of-war, and a one-hundred-yard dash for the annual Bethany Church Sunday school picnic. Later that month he began playing for the Athletics, Foxboro's amateur baseball team. Among the first cut from the Amherst freshman baseball team, Boyden was a non-descript college athlete. But on Foxboro's sandlots he was a hometown hero. "Athletics To Play Sharon August 9," the *Foxboro Reporter* announced, "lineup includes F. Boyden 1st base, batting 2d."

Days before the Sharon game, Boyden received two letters requesting interviews for prospective teaching positions. "One was from a school in Wilton, New Hampshire," Boyden recalled, "the other from Deerfield. Both by coincidence set appointments for the

same day. Unfortunately both were for the day I was to play first base for the Foxboro team. I wrote the schools explaining I had to play a ball game, requesting a later appointment. Wilton wrote me declining another appointment indicating it had no use for baseball players on its faculty. But Deerfield had no objection to first basemen who were short in stature." On the day he might more sensibly have interviewed for a teaching job, Boyden scored two runs on two hits while leading Foxboro to a 10-6 victory over Sharon.

Deerfield had good reason to be less concerned than Wilton about Boyden's preference for baseball. Many Deerfield townspeople had little interest in hiring a truly qualified headmaster. A local newspaper reported popular dissatisfaction with the academy's trustees was so intense that "many who have been the staunchest friends of their school have withdrawn their support preferring rather to see it die than to assist in carrying it on in the way it has been." As one board member said at the time, "It's a toss up whether the academy needs a new headmaster or an undertaker." Some Deerfield folks felt Frank Boyden, an unimpressive five-foot, four-inch, one-hundred-twenty pound, ball-playing "boy" was just the person to close the academy for good.

Desperate for an interview and anxious because the end of the summer was near and teaching opportunities were few, Frank Boyden first walked up Deerfield's unpaved main street on a steamy Tuesday, 12 August 1902. He did not know the complex political web he was stepping into, nor if he did would he have cared. He needed a teaching job and this was his best and perhaps only shot.

Boyden made a positive impression that day. But given town politics and the likelihood no better candidate could be found so late in summer, the interview was a formality. The trustees of Deerfield Academy and Dickinson High School voted him "Principal and Librarian for the ensuing school year at a salary of $800." Boyden promptly accepted the job he would maintain until his retirement in 1968. Arguably the most famous twentieth century American schoolmaster, he raised a poor New England academy to greatness.

2

FOXBORO

Throughout his ninety-three years, Frank Boyden rarely let a week pass without reading the *Foxboro Reporter*. He was fastidious about following the hometown news. "I have been away most of the time for the past two weeks," Boyden once wrote to an editor requesting back issues. "If you have any extra copies I would appreciate your sending them to me. I always look forward to the arrival of the *Reporter* on Saturday."

As Deerfield headmaster, Boyden emphasized the values he learned in his youth. "Foxboro has always meant a great deal to me. As I look back, it seems the young people of our time had a very sane, wholesome, active life. That is just the sort of thing I have tried to give to the boys at Deerfield."

Located in southeastern Massachusetts, Foxboro's tree-lined main streets and white frame buildings center on a public common. Incorporated in 1778 during the American Revolution, Foxboro is named after Charles James Fox, a British member of Parliament who was sympathetic to the colonists. Like Deerfield, Foxboro actively preserves and celebrates its heritage. This is due in part to the local Historical Society Frank Boyden helped establish as an eighteen-year-old. Foxboro's patriotism is reflected in the names of its buildings, the Lincoln Building, Union Block, American House, and Liberty Hall. These structures face the common, where a Civil War soldier stands guard atop a concrete pedestal as he does on a similar monument in Deerfield.

Frank Learoyd Boyden was born in Foxboro to Benjamin Franklin and Anna Wales Cary Boyden on 16 September 1879. Before his birth, the Boydens taught school in nearby Danvers, where they lived with the headmaster's namesake, Deacon Learoyd. "No place seemed

as important in their lives as Danvers," Boyden wrote. "They talked
about it constantly and apparently the happiest years of their lives
were spent there."

With his family growing, Benjamin Boyden quit teaching and
moved to Foxboro, where he could earn a better living as treasurer
of his father-in-law's Foundry and Machine Company. Frank Boyden
spoke infrequently about his parents. He said little about his father
and described his mother as "a gracious and devout religious person,
quiet and a very good Sunday school teacher." But Boyden was
more vocal about Otis Cary, his maternal grandfather, whose
physique, character, energy, and professional accomplishments bear
a striking resemblance to the headmaster's.

At five-feet, six-inches, Cary was familiarly known as "The Little
Man." A horse fanatic as a youth, he regularly drove a team from
the family farm to Boston markets. Stopping along the way to rest
the animals, Cary enjoyed taking short naps, as his grandson did in
later years at Deerfield. Rarely absent from each of two Sunday
school services, Cary was a pious man with great interest in the
temperance and antislavery movements. In 1834 Cary ventured $200
to purchase the Foxboro Foundry. A vigorous businessman well into
his seventies, he is remembered flying about the foundry from task
to task. One day when a visitor inquired for Cary, his employees
replied: "If you hunt for him, you will never find him, but stand in
one place, and within five minutes the Little Man will come around."

As the foundry prospered, Otis Cary bought land. He enjoyed
farming and especially liked haying. He took great interest in politics
and was among Foxboro's first abolitionists. A member of the
Liberty, Republican, and Prohibition parties, he was elected
Foxboro's selectman, assessor, overseer of the poor, state
representative, and state senator. When Foxboro celebrated its
centennial in 1878, Cary presided, as his grandson would do at the
sesquicentennial fifty years later.

Appropriately, the first school Frank Boyden attended was a one
room, eight grade affair named after Otis Cary. There in the Cary
School, a young boy no older than ten, Boyden remembers studying
with "one of the really great teachers in all my educational work."

Like his grandfather, Frank Boyden is fondly remembered for his catnaps, horses, energy, piety, and politics.

The Foxboro of Frank Boyden's youth buzzed with patriotic clubs and progressive reform groups, including the Grand Army of the Republic, Women's Relief Corps, Pilgrim Fathers, Knights of Honor, Golden Cross, and United Workingmen. Among the most active associations, the Independent Order of the Good Templars was a temperance group whose acronym is lightheartedly remembered as standing for "I Often Get Tight." Temperance, however, was not a laughing matter in Foxboro. "There were no liquor stores or saloons in town," according to resident historians Edith and Clifford Lane. "We had local option as we do today. We used to vote on the liquor question on Town Meeting Day. This made quite a lively issue. Very few of the desirable towns voted Yes."

In those days before television, automobiles, and nucleated families, small town life revolved around sociables, skating parties, hay rides, community picnics, and the church. The Lanes remember waking on Sundays in the 1880s to a very full schedule. "The family gathered for morning prayers, some hymns, church, Sunday school, then spent the afternoon driving the 'Democrat,' pulled by the livery stable horse, or calling on the relatives in the late afternoon followed by Junior Endeavor and evening church, and after church, a family sing."

Frank Boyden's Sunday memories corroborate the Lanes's. "A great deal of our life centered on the Congregational Church. I used to go to three services on Sunday. The only reason I didn't go to four is that there wasn't a fourth one. I'm sure of that."

The 1890s brought "progress" to Foxboro in the guise of the Van Choate Electric Company, a manufacturer of electric generators, motors, and incandescent lamps. "This is the age of electricity," the *Reporter* proclaimed. "The demand for supplies in electrical science is continually on the increase. The Van Choate Electric Company is to engage in this line of goods. It stands rapping at our door. Shall we not bid it come in?" In 1894 Foxboro welcomed Van Choate and the thousand jobs it promised. But by the turn of the century, "The bubble is burst. The VCCO has passed into the hands of receivers,

no surprise and small regret. The public is disgusted with the
promoters whose pretensions and promises failed to materialize."

Foxboro's negative experience with Van Choate reaffirmed native
preference for a pastoral ideal. As the Lanes recall, Foxboro
residents were convinced that "farms and small towns had mystic
properties for character building; that village folks were gentler than
city people; that they were closer to God, the land, the brotherhood,
the covenant." Frank Boyden concurred. "My philosophy," he told
John McPhee, "basically is an acceptance of the code of that era."

The 1890s also witnessed the Barton family's arrival in Foxboro.
An esteemed clergyman and noted biographer of Abraham Lincoln,
Reverend William E. Barton moved to town in 1895. As the Barton
family grew, including son Bruce, the celebrated advertising genius
and close Boyden friend, they acquired considerable property between
Granite Street and Lakeview. "The Bartons have kept it up so well,"
Boyden recalled, "that now it is about the best section of Foxboro."

As headmaster, Boyden enjoyed quoting President Lincoln, a
predilection he shared with Dr. Barton. "I like to see a man proud
of the place in which he lives," Boyden often said. "I like to see a
man live so that his place will be proud of him." Boyden and
Barton's loyalty to Foxboro was fierce. "What can we of the present
generation of Foxboro citizens do to make a contribution to the future
worthy of our past?" Barton asked. "I should like to think of
Foxboro as one of the best places in the world for boys and girls to
be born in and which to grow up to manhood and womanhood."
Boyden clearly felt the same way.

On 19 June 1896 Frank Boyden and twelve classmates graduated
from Foxboro High School. Vice president of a class whose motto
was "Attend to the Details," Boyden delivered the commencement
oration. This speech affirming support of Cuba on the brink of the
Spanish-American War was a preliminary expression of Boyden's
lifelong Republican convictions. Boyden was sixteen at the time.
"That's too young," he told McPhee. "I had no competition in high
school, and when I finished I had no interest in education."
Following commencement he went to work for his father driving a
horse and buggy between the train station and the foundry, five trips
a day.

In truth, Boyden was neither too young nor disinterested in further schooling. Foxboro High School had not prepared him sufficiently in foreign languages for admission to college. Boyden consequently began studying French with a tutor. He had his heart set on attending Amherst College, an ambition a devastating fire at the family foundry postponed but did not diminish.

3

AMHERST

In September 1898 Frank Boyden entered Amherst on the eve of a new century. Oil lamps, horses, and farms were on the way out; electricity, automobiles, and cities were on the way in. A progressive age was dawning and Teddy Roosevelt was its "bully" champion. "The last half of the nineteenth century with its marvelous development of business has been increasingly a young man's world," wrote Charles E. Garman, Amherst's revered turn-of-the-century professor. "It is a glorious thing to be a young man at the beginning of the twentieth century. It is your opportunity to make it a college man's world."

Garman's challenge aside, Boyden could barely help himself when he first arrived at Amherst. "I was so green, so small, and so scared I'd be sent home," he said. "I just stayed in my room and worked and worked and worked." Boyden worked so hard in fact that he soon earned the nickname "Plugger Bill." "He was a midnight oil burner," recalls Bob Cleeland. "He was Plugger Bill Boyden. He didn't make an impression on me at all. You stand him up in a line of ten people and try to pick the successful man, you'd pick him tenth."

Boyden interviewed with each of Amherst's eleven fraternities but was not invited back anywhere for the second round. "I was ruled off as a cipher. And it was true. It was a fair judgement. I just boned away everlastingly." He was finally accepted by Phi Kappa Psi. "It was a new fraternity then," said Maynard. "A lot of waifs and strays were taken in there."

Boyden burned the midnight oil, at least until the campus was electrified his senior year, but it was not because Amherst was a rigorous academic institution. According to Professor William

"Biggie" Bigelow, the college between 1890 and 1905 emphasized training the "All-Around Man." "The soul of the boy," he said, "rather than the body or mind, was the object of greatest solicitude."

Dr. Cornelius Patton '83 concurred, "I have always understood that Amherst stood first for a spiritual philosophy as against mere intellectualism. In those days, Amherst was a place of *dolce far niente*, where a meditative youth might sit long on winter evenings before the fire with his fraternity brothers, evolving his crude, inconsistent, but sincere philosophy of life."

Amherst in Boyden's day reflected the attitude and priorities of its president, George Harris. Revered for his humor, Harris was trained for the ministry at Andover Theological Seminary, where he learned a decidedly liberal interpretation of Protestantism. Harris preferred conventional dress to clerical garments while preaching and never talked longer than a half hour. This endeared him to students, who typically were compelled to endure sermons twice as long.

Like Boyden, Harris was not an intellectual. "The educated man is the all-around man, the symmetrical man," Harris said. "The aim of a college is not to make scholars. The aim is to make broad, cultivated men, physically sound, intellectually awake, socially refined and gentlemanly, with appreciation of art, music, literature, and with sane, simple religion, all in proportion, not athletes simply, not scholars simply, not dilettantes, not society men, not pietists, but all-round men."

At Deerfield, Boyden shared Harris's emphasis on educating the all-around man. "The success this school has had," Boyden said in later years, "has been due to thorough grounding not only in basic academics but, almost more important, in training boys' attitudes toward life which will persist long after the precise details of booktraining have dimmed." Boyden enjoyed quoting Gifford Pinchot, a Roosevelt New Dealer, on this subject: "Half a century of experience in executive work has proved to me that the first condition of success in any job is not brains but character. Over and over I have seen men of moderate intelligence come to the front because they had courage, integrity, self-respect, steadiness, perseverance, and confidence in themselves, their cause, and their work."

There is little doubt President Harris's popularity at Amherst was amplified by his wife's presence. Like Helen Boyden, who was crucial to Deerfield's success, Mrs. Harris was the president's equal in Amherst students' estimation. This was particularly true when she reintroduced dancing to campus after a long period of lingering suppression. "Although Mrs. Harris was insistent on etiquette and formality," Claude Fuess writes, "she knew how to make timid youth feel at home."

If Boyden's Amherst was not a rigorous intellectual institution, it was a place where physical fitness and athletic participation mattered disproportionately. In 1859 Amherst played Williams in America's first intercollegiate baseball game. The following year Amherst established the nation's first physical education program. "It is to Amherst College," President Eliot of Harvard once said, "that the colleges of the country are indebted for a demonstration of the proper method of organizing the Department of Physical Education."

Appointed professor of Hygiene and Physical Education in 1861, a position he held for fifty years, Dr. Edward Hitchcock was the genius behind the program, a man whose influence on Amherst alumni was enormous. "Old Doc" Hitchcock was the son of a former Deerfield headmaster and Amherst College president. A pioneer in the field of anthropometry, the science directed toward both quantifying and maximizing physical development through statistically monitored exercise, Doc Hitchcock's novel gymnastics program drew visitors and professional observers to Amherst from all over the world.

Hitchcock was "brisk and breezy and tireless," according to Claude Fuess, "impatient with effeminacy in young men, blunt in speech and manner." But behind Doc's gruff intimidating exterior was a kind, understanding soul who as dean during Boyden's years "knew every undergraduate and his idiosyncracies and was so full of the milk of kindness that he always was ready to give a delinquent a second chance." It is not difficult to see Old Doc's influence on Frank Boyden. Two of the headmaster's most celebrated attributes, required athletics for all and a flair for working with boys who had failed at other institutions, come directly from the Hitchcock textbook.

Harris and Hitchcock made an indelible impression on Frank Boyden. But Professor George Olds became his lifelong friend. Like Boyden, Olds had been a schoolteacher and headmaster of a private academy at Albany, New York. After Albany, Olds taught mathematics first at the University of Rochester, then at Amherst, where he became dean and president.

Boyden and Olds had much in common, not the least of which was their diminutive physical size. Like Boyden, Olds was "small of stature, bespectacled, and rather frail in physique," according to Fuess. "But he soon revealed himself as an inspiring instructor who could make algebra as romantic as Kubla Khan. His red hair and nervous gestures led the undergraduates to christen him the Rochester Burner. With a genius for winning and retaining friends, he became one of the three most popular faculty members, not because he was easy, but because he was just and sympathetic."

When Olds announced his retirement from teaching in 1926, he exchanged letters with Boyden. This correspondence reveals their mutual respect and admiration. "I find it impossible to express to you in any way the deep appreciation which we all feel for what you have done for the college and the real love which we bear to you personally," Boyden wrote. "I wish you could know how much the inspiration I have received from you has contributed to the work I have been trying to do at Deerfield."

Olds's reply to Boyden speaks for itself. "Few men among our graduates have been so completely incarnated with the fundamental idea of Amherst College as have you. I have received many tributes in the way of appreciation within the last month, but surely there is no word which could possibly give me greater satisfaction than what you say as to my contribution toward your success at Deerfield."

It is hard to imagine a professor who had greater influence on Boyden than Edward Hitchcock or George Olds. But Charles Garman did. Speaking at the 1902 commencement, David Keedy asked the audience to "pause in silent reverence to hear our humble tribute to a great man, Charles E. Garman. For the highest and best that Amherst has given us we have him to thank. He has given us higher ideals, broader visions, noble purposes. The characters we take into the world have felt the touch of the master hand. Though

years pass and the cares of a busy life press hard upon us, yet amid the din and strife of a bustling world . . . we will hear that soft and silvery voice, earnestly pledging the cause of right and duty."

Sixty-five years later on the eve of yet another Amherst '02 reunion, Garman's influence remained powerful as ever. "I haven't looked up the statistics as to how much other members of 1902 have over the years contributed to those places and positions in which it has pleased God to put them," Jack Frizzell wrote on behalf of his Class. "But this I do know, the contribution has been both large and significant. And why? I like to think we have been guided and inspired by the example and the teaching of our beloved Charlie Garman."

Born in Maine in 1850 to an orthodox Congregational minister, Charles Edward Garman graduated from Amherst in 1872. Like Olds and Boyden, Garman's career began as a high school principal. But after four years teaching at Ware, Massachusetts, he opted for Yale Divinity School and then for an initial position at Amherst as a mathematics instructor. Garman soon shifted to the philosophy department, the discipline in which he was most adept and interested.

A bright but not brilliant thinker, Garman's genius stemmed from his compelling teaching style and his infinite patience and generosity. Throughout his twenty-seven Amherst years, Garman's door was always open to visitors, especially on Saturday evenings when students regularly gathered as Deerfield boys did at the Boydens' in later years. According to Thomas Le Duc, Garman "had no illusions about the charm of high abstractions for the average young man. To attract students' attention, he drew eclectically on all likely material, whether historical, topical, or clinical. He adapted himself skillfully to the changing interests of his students."

While most instruction in Garman's day emphasized mastery of a specific academic subject, his teaching concentrated on inspiring students' civic consciousness and sense of public responsibility. Whether in class or out, Garman never missed an opportunity to advance this ethic of public stewardship. "Every term, every lecture, almost every word was really a lesson in ethics, a sermon on the categorical imperative," one of his students recalls. "That every man has an intuitive perception of virtue and a transcending obligation to

follow its command, Garman labored every day to establish as the deepest conviction of his students."

If a teacher is best judged by the accomplishments of his students, the distinguished public service of Harlan Stone, Calvin Coolidge, Dwight Morrow, Joseph B. Eastman, and Frank Boyden himself, to name only the most prominent of Garman's pupils, certainly reflect well on this remarkable man. Boyden regarded Charlie Garman as "one of the greatest teachers in America." He admired his mentor's loyalty to Amherst. "Garman could have had deanships and presidencies elsewhere," Boyden said. "But he preferred to stay right at Amherst and send people like Morrow out to do their work in the world." The same might be said of Boyden, who declined many lucrative job offers over his sixty-six-year Deerfield tenure.

Frank Boyden may have been an introverted "grind" when he first arrived at Amherst, but it did not take him long to make at least one lifelong friend in Bob Maynard who stands beside him in the freshman class photograph. If Boyden was not the most popular, handsome, congenial, or brilliant member of his class, he at least had the good sense to associate with Maynard who was. This intuitive knack for cultivating advantageous associations was one of Boyden's greatest attributes.

Bob Maynard was born in Newport, Rhode Island, to Admiral Washburn and Mary Brooks Maynard. Second in his class and Phi Beta Kappa at Amherst, he managed the basketball team and had the necessary fortitude, sense of humor, and virility to play the female lead in the senior class play. For his efforts, Maynard was chosen class prophet, a responsibility he fulfilled at the senior banquet by announcing, "The best Prophecy of the future is the past." This conservative conviction was not unlike Deerfield's motto, "Be Worthy of Your Heritage."

A graduate of Harvard Law and the president of R.H. Stearns, a prominent Boston retailer, Maynard would serve over fifty years on Deerfield's Board of Trustees and nearly as many on Amherst's. In 1968 the academy recognized him with its highest honor, a Deerfield Medal: "For over seventy years you have been the man behind the man. As a devoted friend of 'Bill' Boyden and of Deerfield, you have given unstintingly of your time, often at great personal sacrifice,

to offer wise counsel and needed encouragement. You, sir, are a great gentleman whom we all love and admire."

Boyden knew Maynard through their mutual interest in debate. Both were members of the Hardy 16, along with another Boyden friend, Eugene "Tug" Wilson. Unlike his more cerebral friends, Tug made his mark as an Amherst athlete. Captain of one of the best track teams in the college's history and one of Amherst's all-time hurdlers, Wilson led his squad to the New England championship and a fourth place finish in the national competition.

Like Boyden, Wilson taught high school at Smith Academy in St. Louis, where he also began studying law at Washington University. He soon dropped teaching for a business career that culminated in his appointment as general counsel and vice president of American Telephone and Telegraph. Putting his financial and legal acumen as well as his extensive business connections to good use, Wilson later played a vital role building the endowments of both Amherst and Deerfield.

The change Amherst wrought in Frank Boyden was significant. By senior year, the once reclusive young man had organized Amherst's first intramural and intercollegiate tennis programs, a harbinger of things to come at Deerfield, which prides itself among secondary schools and small colleges for its outstanding tennis. At commencement, Boyden's classmates voted him second as "the man whom the college has benefitted most."

On 10 June 1902, his Amherst years nearly done, his future uncertain, Frank Boyden sat in chapel where Professor Anson Morse addressed the graduating class. "Success is making things better," Morse said. "To leave things as we find them is to accomplish nothing; to make them worse is to fail." Frank Boyden's life's work would corroborate this broad definition of success.

4

REVIVAL

Deerfield legend has it Frank Boyden was met at the academy's front door by a handful of young men intent on destroying him. According to John McPhee, "Of the seven boys in the academy when he took over in 1902 at least four were regarded with fear." These youth were so frightening, "it had been the habit of people of Deerfield to cross the street before passing the academy."

The facts of Boyden's Deerfield tenure, especially in these early years, are obscured by myths Boyden often cultivated himself. R. W. Sibley, who preceded Boyden as headmaster, had a different story about these allegedly incorrigible kids. "The discipline of the school you will find easy," Sibley wrote Boyden on the eve of his first day's work. "The children are all amiable. I am fond of them all."

Boyden's task, however, would not be easy. Although Sibley was an able man who later became dean of the Cornell English Department, he had his hands full at Deerfield. "The school is small," Sibley continued, "it would be foolishness to expect a remarkable average of achievements. Indeed you will probably begin, as I did, with a disgusted wonder at your predecessor and the little he put in his pupils' heads; you may end, as I did, with compassion and respect for him."

Mastering Deerfield students was not Boyden's only challenge. Responding to adults engaged in a bitter dispute over trustee mismanagement of the academy was an equally daunting task that Sibley avoided altogether. "It is not surprising to know that I kept out of politics," Sibley told Boyden. "The intricacies of Deerfield politics I shall not attempt to explain: you will know volumes in a few weeks."

Residents of western Massachusetts were quite familiar with the unsavory details of Deerfield politics. "Deerfield school affairs are only the result of the moral degeneracy of the whole town," the *Springfield Republican* reported in 1900. "Politics, social life, and religion are on a low level. There are a few splendid people there, but many of them have suffered by being depressed at the general condition."

Discord over Deerfield schools originated in 1876 with the problematic union of Deerfield Academy and the public high school. This merger occurred when the town received a bequest from Esther Dickinson for a new public high school and library. Welcome as the new Dickinson High School was for the town, it posed an immediate dilemma for the historic but venerable private academy since Deerfield was too small to support two secondary schools.

Founded in 1797, Deerfield Academy had been one of the first and finest private schools in the early American Republic. In those days before public schools, when a college education was the exception and not the rule, academies were considered essential for training the citizens and civic leaders vital to America's nascent democracy.

No town was better suited for an American academy than Deerfield. Situated in the Connecticut River Valley beside a gravelly tributary, Deerfield is enfolded between hills to the east and west. A seventeenth century frontier outpost, Deerfield once stood alone at the northwesternmost corner of the colonies, where it bravely survived French and Mohawk attacks.

When the seventeenth century turned and the frontier passed to New York, Deerfield became one of the most appealing residences in Massachusetts. With a moderate climate by New England standards and superior soil for growing corn, onions, beans, and tobacco and for fattening cattle, eighteenth century Deerfield became Hampshire County's commercial and cultural hub.

Deerfield Academy prospered in the early nineteenth century under the direction of Edward Hitchcock, an eminent paleontologist and future Amherst College president. But westward expansion and industrialization undercut Deerfield's regional influence. Families once bound for Deerfield began to bypass it for Greenfield, Springfield, Hartford, Pittsfield, and Albany. Though still a good

school, Deerfield Academy was challenged by rival academies situated near these rapidly growing population centers. Even more ominous, popular sentiment favoring a national system of public schools threatened the viability of all private academies.

By 1876, the year of Dickinson's $70,000 bequest for the new high school, Deerfield Academy's assets totaled $18,000. Its enrollment had dwindled to few more than a dozen. Since the town could not support two high schools, the academy trustees voted to merge with Dickinson High School. In 1877, the Massachusetts legislature approved the new corporation named "the Trustees of the Deerfield Academy and Dickinson High School." A handsome new school building with physical and chemical laboratories, music room, assembly hall, and library was built and dedicated in 1878.

For several years Deerfield Academy and Dickinson High School prospered. This was due to its first principals, J. Y. Bergin, who later became a well-known physicist, and W. Starr Cutting, subsequently an associate professor of modern languages at the University of Chicago. But by the end of the century, Deerfield Academy and Dickinson High School had fallen on such hard times that an agent for the state board of education said "Deerfield Academy can not be called a fair equivalent for a high school." Dissatisfied with local education, Deerfield families began to send their children to nearby Greenfield instead.

In January 1899 the centennial anniversary of the original Deerfield Academy passed uncelebrated. When the *Springfield Republican* investigated this omission, a Deerfield Academy and Dickinson High School alumnus said "It was not wise to attract to the institution the interest and support which would follow a celebration while it was controlled by a board whose management is openly questioned."

The Deerfield and Dickinson trustees had little apparent concern for quality instruction. They seemed equally negligent about school finances. Although they refused to insure the school against fire, they voted themselves salaries for a task typically undertaken gratis. "In most institutions of this character," the *Republican* reported, "there are enough men in the community who are willing to give their services as trustees that the funds may be husbanded for the

maintenance of the school. The sum [paid for the salaries] is not large to be sure, but it shows the spirit of grab [in Deerfield] which is astonishing."

The board responsible for the school's decline was headed by P.D. Bridges. It included C. E. Williams, Captain Ephraim Williams, and B. Z. Stebbins, Jr., all of Deerfield, and Rev. Andrew Campbell, of Webster. To his credit, Campbell was publicly acknowledged as a staunch and consistent "minority member of the board who is not in sympathy with the present regime." A vocal dissenter, Campbell was run out of town for his objections to board policy.

Citing Campbell's confrontation with Bridges, Sibley warned Boyden about the occupational hazards of local politics. "The foundation of the trouble was laid a few years ago by the Unitarian minister 'we' say. He tried to 'reform' the town. Major Bridges, Chairman of the Trustees, led the forces on the other side. The Major is still leading. The Unitarian minister is not. He has left town. I think it may go so far as to say that it is safe, and well-nigh always sensible, to agree with Major Bridges."

Teaching school was easy compared to surviving such cutthroat local politics. But talented schoolmaster that Frank Boyden was, he was an equally skillful politician. Boyden did not intend to avoid Deerfield politics, nor would he cowtow to Bridges. At Amherst, Charlie Garman had challenged him to stand for the right and the good. That was exactly what Boyden intended to do.

Boyden was not alone in the battle. He had a dedicated ally and kindred spirit in Andrew Campbell, who had remained an academy trustee despite Bridges's best efforts to remove him. Born in Cambridge in 1870, Campbell attended Phillips Andover Academy and Yale Divinity School before accepting his first pastorate at Deerfield. Boyden admitted he could not have tackled Bridges successfully without Campbell's assistance. "The present position of the Academy in the educational world is due very largely to his untiring efforts," Boyden said. "It was a trying experience for all of us and I don't think anyone will ever realize how much real responsibility Andrew took."

Soon after Campbell and Boyden began rallying support for Deerfield Academy and Dickinson High School, the *Republican*

joined the fight. "While the recent history of Deerfield Academy and Dickinson High School is not a pleasant chapter, there are people in Deerfield capable of managing the affairs of the institution in a manner above reproach. Let this come. Bossism has been overthrown before."

Quoting President Lincoln, Frank Boyden believed: "Public sentiment is everything. With public sentiment, nothing can fail; without it, nothing can succeed." In the fall of 1902, restoring the town's confidence in Deerfield Academy and Dickinson High School was first on Boyden's political and pedagogical agenda. When Boyden first arrived in Deerfield, Dumont Lamb, a Deerfield and Dickinson junior, described the school as "weak in spirit and under the ban of public disapproval." When Lamb graduated in 1904, he left "seeing all about us signs of renewed life." The positive change Boyden wrought in Deerfield Academy and Dickinson High School was immediate and dramatic.

A young man of twenty-four who taught because he could not afford law school, Boyden had a natural gift as an educator. Within months this untested rookie was both articulating and implementing an educational vision worthy of a seasoned veteran. "We believe that education includes more than the mental training of the school room," he wrote near the end of the first year, using words reminiscent of George Harris. "Every effort should be made to develop the scholars physically and morally."

Like Amherst under Harris, Boyden's Deerfield emphasized an all-around education. In class, Boyden taught physical geography and the algebra he'd learned from George Olds. Out of class, Boyden gained student interest and respect through ample doses of athletics. "Football, basketball, and baseball for the boys and basketball for the girls," he said. "Through these games the recreation time is spent in an orderly systematic manner. The pupils are brought into relation with one another and the teacher and much spirit is caused among all."

It is not certain if Boyden "broke" a recalcitrant six-foot farm boy on the first day of school. Deerfield lore says the two stood nearly toe-to-toe, hurling a baseball back and forth, catching it barehanded until the boy finally begged off, his hand swollen shut. But it is

certain the boys played ball every afternoon after classes. And the principal himself, fresh from Foxboro's sandlots, joined in.

Boyden wasted no time organizing a football team and scheduling games against Greenfield High and Amherst College. Deerfield lost the Greenfield game 48-0 but Lamb was not discouraged. "Although the score stood against us, we all came home that night filled with determination to win from our friends across the river, sometime."

A memorable reception followed the Amherst contest. Deerfield and Dickinson girls served lunch. Amherst men sang college songs. "It was at this time," Lamb remembers, "we first realized the value of school songs and cheers in keeping up a good, lively school spirit." Proud of its glee club, which was among the oldest in New England, Amherst always had been a strong singing school just as Boyden intended Deerfield would be.

"School" did not end at Deerfield Academy and Dickinson High School when the books were put away. At Amherst, Boyden's once introverted, book-bound life was enriched by his involvement in fraternity and college life at-large. At Deerfield and Dickinson, Boyden strived to develop the school's social dimension as well. "It was in this year that our school life began to be more pleasant," Lamb recalls. "For we now saw that it had a social side and that the advantages to be gained in this were as important in their place as those gained in books and study. Early in the fall we voted to hold class meetings each month at the home of the different members. We spent an evening with each classmate in this way, enjoying ourselves more and more at each successive meeting as we all became better acquainted." By enlisting the help of local families in this endeavor, Boyden began to impress them firsthand with his earnestness, dedication, and vision.

School spirit was high when winter brought basketball season and "the most exciting expedition of the year," a horse-drawn, Boyden-led sleigh ride along the Mill River Road. "Although there were only eight in the party, it was not a noiseless one. Our melodious voices were accompanied by a tin horn and at intervals our 'DA, DA' came in very usefully." As they passed through the meadows south of town, Lamb recalls, "I think we must have waked up Gabriel, for we heard a trumpet call in answer to our own."

Spring meant baseball, Boyden's favorite pastime. And when the Deerfield and Dickinson nine took the field, the headmaster stood at first base in full uniform, mitt in hand. Spring, too, brought a dramatic presentation as part of Boyden's grand scheme to keep students happily busy while concurrently entertaining local townspeople.

The joyful twenty-fifth anniversary of the Deerfield Academy and Dickinson High School merger was a testament to Boyden's first year achievement. Only four years earlier, Deerfield alumni had refused to recognize the academy's centennial, hoping instead the school would fade from memory if not from existence. Now, the tide of public sentiment flooded in the school's favor.

On 12 June 1903 the festivities began with a 2:00 baseball game. A reception and a meeting to reorganize the alumni association followed. "With the idea of prosecuting a vigorous campaign in the interest of the school," the reconstituted association elected Boyden's Amherst mentor, Doc Hitchcock, president. It then proposed raising $1,000 to refurnish the school's physics and chemistry labs. At 7:00 three hundred people assembled in Dickinson Hall for an alumni dinner and presentation of diplomas to the two graduating seniors. Amherst President George Harris was the commencement speaker.

On this occasion the Greenfield *Recorder* reported, "DHS at Deerfield observed in a happy manner its 25th anniversary, bringing together a large company of the friends and alumni of the school, who by their presence and expressions of interest inaugurated what is expected to be a revival of that institution which in years past has stood finest among the academies of the state." In his first year as headmaster, Frank Boyden had rejuvenated a school once written off as dead.

5

COMMUNITY CENTER

By building a school the Deerfield community believed in, the young headmaster was gaining more influence and respect than any local legislator. Once secure in his position, Boyden planned to direct his power against P. D. Bridges, the incumbent political boss and academy trustee.

Boyden's primary power base was his students and their parents. Although academy legend exaggerates the initial adversarial relationship between the headmaster and his charges, little evidence supports such tension. Throughout his career, Boyden had great confidence in the fundamental goodness of youth. "I want to reaffirm my faith in the teenager," he once said. "I get awfully fed up with those people who are constantly asserting that our young people are going or have already gone completely to the dogs, because they simply don't know what they are talking about."

Boyden's primary model for Deerfield was an idealized conception of the family. "Most of all I believe in the home, the home environment, and more time spent together as a family," he said. "Seek to develop in your children traits of character, and personality, intellect, a sense of public relations and the will to succeed. If we can do this we will be all right."

When confronted with a difficult youth, Boyden preferred to reason with and understand him rather than whip him into shape as Endicott Peabody did at the Groton School. Boyden could no sooner expel a problematic student than a parent could dismiss a wayward child. Before long, Deerfield earned a reputation as a welcome haven where boys who had failed at other private schools might save face and make good on a second chance.

Although he envisioned Deerfield Academy and Dickinson High School as an extended family, Boyden did not cast himself as the dominating patriarch. Unlike several rival prep schools that consciously imitate aristocratic English public schools like Eton or Rugby, Deerfield is considered among the most democratic and therefore "American" private schools. This is a credit to Boyden's leadership, which was deeply rooted in his ability to convince students to want to do for themselves what he himself implicitly demanded they do.

In 1902 Boyden challenged his fourteen students, "I believe we can make this the best school in Franklin County. It will be your school and nobody else's if you do." By 1904 the graduating class believed they had met Boyden's challenge. "This Academy belongs to us as it can to no other class. We began our course here when only a few would come, and numbers were needed. We entered a large class, and we go out a larger class than has been graduated from this institution for many years. We found the school weak in spirit and under the ban of public disapproval. We leave it now seeing all about us signs of renewed life." Typically humble and self-effacing, Boyden deferred personal credit for this achievement, casting it instead on the students and alumni where it served more good.

As much as Boyden cared about his students and delegated responsibility for self-improvement, the headmaster ultimately succeeded because he made school fun. "Education," Boyden said, "requires faith, hope, charity and most of all a sense of humor." This is why the headmaster cherished this letter from a Connecticut boy who wrote him prior to entering the academy: "The social life around New Canaan has been very active. I'd like to know whether Deerfield has any social activities and, if so, what? Every week end we get together and dance, play games, go to the movies, or bowl. We (our ninth grade 'gang') like to get together either by parties or by going to the movies. All in all, it is fun, which is the way God meant it."

Fun came in many forms at Deerfield, but athletics was its most obvious and popular guise. Boyden recalls those first years. "We had an hour and a half noon hour and recess periods in the morning and afternoon. During those times the scholars got into no end of

trouble. We cut down the noon hour to forty minutes, so that we had time at the end of the day for recreation. The boys were divided into three squads, and every boy had one form of athletic work every day." Before long Boyden's athletic program paid noticeable dividends both for the students and the town. Deerfield athletics fast became a source of local entertainment and civic pride, especially when the 1904 basketball and baseball teams upset "big-city" rival Greenfield High School.

Boyden liked to tell this story about one of his first fund-raising achievements. "After about two years an interesting lady who comes to Deerfield for the summers asked if there was anything I would like some money for use in my school work. I suppose she thought I might like an encyclopedia, or a dictionary, or something of that sort. I looked out for a couple of minutes and I wondered if I dared ask her for the thing I wanted most. Finally I did. I asked her for baseball uniforms. She looked back at me a few minutes and wondered if she dared say yes. Finally she said, 'Well, something has made a change in the young people in Deerfield, and if you say it is athletics, you may buy the uniforms, but don't ever mention my name.'" The lady's name was Jenny Sheldon and the uniforms were the first of her many generous gifts to the academy.

In addition to athletics, Boyden believed in sponsoring school parties. Then as now, partying youth posed a troublesome problem for parents and school alike. Much to everyone's satisfaction, Boyden had a solution. "There was the question of parties," he said. "Some of the children had a party on Tuesday night, some Wednesday night, and some Thursday night, so that every morning there was a good proportion of the school tired and unsuited for school work. We asked the parents to keep the boys and girls home except Friday nights, and said we would go ourselves to the Friday night parties. We were looked askance at in the beginning but when we arranged for something to do we became welcome. We play games, and afterwards put out the lights and light the fire and sit around our big old fireplace and sing songs and tell stories. There is something about it that draws them together and that makes for school spirit and loyalty that seems almost impossible to get in any other way."

Despite Boyden's personal distaste for dancing, Deerfield Academy and Dickinson High School proms became much anticipated, buoyantly celebrated town-wide affairs. "I never danced a step in my life," Boyden said. "I was brought up to believe dancing was the work of the devil and I guess it is sometimes. The children were attending public dances, and we wanted to stop it, but it was useless to say they couldn't go, so we decided to run our own high school dances We went to the best people in town and said, 'Now, you want things to run better in this town. Come to these high school receptions and make the boys and girls feel they are the best and biggest in town.' They came and now we have a receiving line sometimes of from fifty to seventy-five people. The class giving the reception meet them formally first, and then introduce the rest of the scholars, thereby gaining ease and poise which some of us born in the country often wish we had more chance to acquire."

Deerfield drama provided yet another fun activity and constructive means of controlling students and winning public favor. "In some way we had to get the people interested in the academy. We had to advertise. So we put on a play whenever we heard there was anything going on that we didn't want the boys to go to, we called a rehearsal of the play for that night. Well, we knew that play thoroughly and gave it twice, and to over six hundred people."

Through athletics, parties, dances, and drama, Deerfield Academy and Dickinson High School became a vital community center that bound Deerfield together at a time when centripetal forces like automobiles, cities, and heavy industry threatened to fracture it irrevocably. "I want to talk to you tonight about the country high school," Boyden said in a speech to the American Playground Recreation Commission. It is "the logical social center because it is the one institution that can get all the young people of the town together without any denominational or sectional differences. Conditions in the country are changing. It is much easier for people to go than it used to be. Trolleys, automobiles, and such things have tended to break down the influence of the home. Times are changing in the country, and somebody has got to right things up. The high school seems to be the most powerful force to accomplish this end."

6

LOCAL POLITICS

Except for his daily glance at the Bible and his weekly review of the *Foxboro Reporter*, Boyden had little time for reading. But there was one book by the historical novelist Winston Churchill that he recommended with unusual zeal. "Have you by any chance read *Coniston*?" Boyden wrote George Goodell, a former Deerfield Academy and Dickinson High School principal. "If not, I urge you to get a copy from the library and do so for it describes exactly the political situation that existed here under Major Bridges."

Set in a New Hampshire hill town not unlike Deerfield, *Coniston* chronicles the unlikely rise of a country tanner named Jethro Bass to statewide political power. The resemblance between Bass and Boyden is striking. Both men were unremarkable in physical stature. Both were exceptionally ambitious. Both enjoyed a preference for crackers at breakfast, although Bass took them with milk and Boyden preferred root beer.

"Mark my words," a Coniston townsman announces much as a Deerfield citizen might have said of Boyden, "Jethro Bass is an all-fired sight smarter than folks in this town think he be. They don't take notice of him, because he don't say much . . . But I wouldn't be afeard to warrant he'd make a racket in the world some of these days." *Coniston* tells the story of Bass's tangle with railroad magnate and rival political boss Isaac Worthington. "This town's tired of puttin' up with a king," Bass says of his antagonist. "It's time to stop this one man rule. You kin go tell him I said it." In 1903 Boyden felt similarly about P. D. Bridges when the battle for control of Deerfield Academy and Dickinson High School began in earnest.

After one year with Boyden at the helm, Deerfield and Dickinson enrollment had tripled to forty-three students. This growth created

an immediate fiscal problem since the annual income from the
Dickinson bequest was insufficient to meet the cost of educating
more students. To compound matters, the school's endowment
suffered a substantial loss when Greenfield's Packard National Bank
defaulted on an unsecured Dickinson deposit.

For years Deerfield Academy and Dickinson High School had
defrayed the cost of transporting students to the semiprivate school
by appropriating public money at town meeting. But now, with
many more students enrolled, most of whom lived on the distant
south side of town, transportation costs had increased dramatically.
Several townspeople, Bridges among them, balked at this growing
transportation subsidy. They argued no further public money should
be allocated to Deerfield and Dickinson until its management was
transferred from a private board of trustees to the town's
superintendent of schools, P. D. Bridges himself.

While Boyden worked feverishly behind the scenes, John J.
Greenough publicly championed opposition to Bridges. A thoughtful,
honest farmer with strong convictions and few reservations about
expressing them, Greenough would become a close Boyden friend,
as well as the subject of one of the headmaster's favorite stories.

"Many years ago," as Boyden told it, "one of the leading citizens
of the town was Deacon Greenough. He had many interests, and
among them was a horseradish plant. Every year at Thanksgiving
time he used to drive down to school in his horse and buggy, and
give to each boy to take home a bottle of horseradish in a yellow
carton. Bear in mind that his name was Greenough and that on the
side of the carton was a large 'O' in green ink. On the other side it
said, 'If a young man likes a young woman, that's his business; if
a young woman likes a young man, that's her business; but if they
both like horseradish . . . that's my business.'" Boyden always
finished this story by adding, "If we are truly interested in education,
that's our business."

In 1903 John Greenough made it his business to defend Deerfield
Academy and Dickinson High School against those who hoped to
transfer the school entirely to the public domain. In his first major
sally, Greenough chastised the board for its neglect of the South
Deerfield grammar school. A recent fire in an adjacent building had

heightened public concern about the school's deteriorating physical condition. When the building was condemned pending replacement of its furnace and other mandated repairs, Bridges did nothing.

Bridges's indifference prompted Greenough to notify the state building inspector, who ordered the town to bring the school up to code or close it down. Greenough next solicited architectural drawings for the required work and presented a bill for $18.90. Bridges did the same but charged $113.24. Bridges also requested $263.00 for services he had rendered as acting superintendent of schools. Greenough contested this work was already salaried at $85.00.

Bridges believed the South Deerfield school building was "a creditable structure, well-equipped, with few equals in the surrounding towns of our size for pupils of similar grades." Even if renovation was necessary, the school committee was having difficulty meeting daily operating expenses without making additional capital improvements. "As it was found that we should not have funds enough to procure the heater and continue our schools at the desired time, we consequently postponed the purchase of the heater." Bridges berated Greenough for blowing the whistle on his home town. "If the State Inspector was to be called to every school and public building in town, by some one who wanted to make a newspaper item, we should have to mortgage our farms to meet the expenses."

But these issues were peripheral to the debate over using public money to subsidize transporting students to a semiprivate academy. Greenough based his argument on historical precedent. "We remind you that ever since the founding of the High School in 1878 the town has appropriated money for the benefit of the institution in accordance with the will of Mrs. Dickinson, and no question of the legality of the town's action arose until 1903." For over twenty-five years the town had consistently voted money for the school. The school committee was required by law to act on this vote. It had no authority to obstruct the public will. "This much we have on the best authority that the state will take no action to prevent us from appropriating money for this purpose, if we desire to do so, and that it is the duty of the committee as servant of the town to carry out

votes passed at the annual meeting instead of sitting down and quibbling over the legality of said votes."

Bridges countered with the opinion of a former secretary of the state Board of Education. "If the institution known as Deerfield Academy and Dickinson High School is not under the order of superintendence of the school committee of Deerfield, then the Town of Deerfield has no right to expend any money upon it." Bridges proposed transferring the academy to the town so it could draw a generous share of the state funds allocated to public high schools. Not coincidentally, this transfer would also augment Bridges's authority as superintendent of schools.

Churchill's *Coniston* begins with a citation from James Russell Lowell: "Popular government is no better than any other form except as the virtue and wisdom of the people make it so." In this first battle for control of Deerfield Academy and Dickinson High School, the Deerfield people supported Boyden over Bridges. Reassured by state authorities that town appropriations for the school were permissible, the divisive matter was put to rest at least for the moment. According to the Greenfield *Gazette*, "The fact that the school is prospering as it has not prospered for years is indication that the present solution is the best that it could be." There was little reason to meddle with such success.

As good a schoolmaster as Boyden was, the young headmaster had more ambition than a classroom or school full of children alone could reasonably satisfy. From the outset, Boyden considered the Deerfield and Dickinson principalship a political as well as a pedagogical challenge. Boyden realized reviving the academy was a matter not so much of improved instruction as it was an issue of winning public confidence. Although he originally signed on at Deerfield for but a year or two, Boyden was soon revered as a local hero. He had also tasted the surprisingly sweet spoils of political victory. In 1904 few of Boyden's Amherst peers could boast of such an achievement.

HELEN CHILDS

Public acclaim and political fortune compelled Boyden to linger in Deerfield longer than he had planned. Love for a local girl laid permanent roots. In 1905 Boyden hired Helen Childs as a mathematics and science teacher, warning her lest there be any doubt, "If you ever have any trouble with the boys, remember that I'll be on the other side." How little Boyden knew then about this woman who shared his knack for understanding and motivating students, this woman who would soon be his wife.

As much as Frank Boyden accomplished at Deerfield, his achievement would have been impossible without Helen Childs. "Without you the Head could never have performed the wonders he has," Bruce Barton, Jr., wrote. "Nor would any of us have quite the same love for the school that we have. In the background of all our lives is the memory of your enthusiasm, your wit, your kindness, and your generosity."

Helen Sears Childs was born in Deerfield to Theodore and Clara Childs on 20 September 1883. Her father was a wealthy dairy farmer, highway contractor, and bridge builder. Childs prepared for admission to nearby Smith College. But because her parents disapproved of the education offered at Deerfield Academy and Dickinson High School, she studied at Greenfield High, where she graduated in 1900. The class motto that year was "Live to Learn," an imperative no classmate exemplified better than Helen Childs.

At Smith, Childs distinguished herself as a mathematics student and secretary of the Math Club. But she was no book-bound drone. A voracious reader and inquisitive student, Childs relished attending meetings of the colloquium and the current events club, where

debates on contemporary progressive issues were both frequent and animated.

According to Charlotte Burgis DeForest, Childs's college classmate, Smith endeavored before all else to cultivate the ideal of "intellectual womanliness." This involved a delicate balance between mental acuity and gentle femininity. Helen Childs personified this ideal. A precise, exacting teacher with a firm command of her discipline, she also had enormous faith, kindness, humor, and understanding. Remembered as Deerfield's greatest teacher, she also had the biggest heart.

Helen Childs was the first to admit she was no physical beauty. "I don't like pictures," she once said, "they show what I look like." In later years, one reporter wrote Childs "looked more like Eleanor Roosevelt than Raquel Welch. But there were some of us who thought of Helen Childs as beautiful. She had large ears and yet she always wore her hair high on her head, pinned usually in little buns at the crown. Her nose, and there is no more delicate way to put it, was proportionately large for her face. But Helen Boyden was beautiful because she had eyes like Helen Hayes, and she had a compelling way about her."

After graduating from Smith, Childs taught at the Catherine Aiken School in Stamford, Connecticut. But with her father terminally ill, she returned to Deerfield. When Theodore died, Childs opted to remain in Deerfield to teach mathematics at Deerfield Academy and Dickinson High School. She married the headmaster two years later.

Frank Boyden and Helen Childs exchanged vows on 27 June 1907. That Thursday evening the wedding party left the Childs's home in Deerfield's Wapping district and arrived by chartered trolley at the Old Unitarian Church. Hundreds gathered to witness the marriage performed by Rev. Andrew Campbell. According to the Greenfield *Recorder*, a reception followed in the school building where "groups of Smith and Amherst College mates of the couple alternated in singing and cheering for the bride and bridegroom. At 9:00 the family returned to Wapping and the happy couple travelled to Springfield by automobile. It was the first ride in an automobile for either of them, adding excitement to their day. After a honeymoon month in Duxbury, they visited Foxboro and returned to Deerfield."

By marrying into one of the oldest and wealthiest families in town, Frank Boyden bound his fortune more closely to Deerfield. In recognition of the Boyden union, Deerfield townspeople collected a sum of money for the newlyweds and presented it to the bridegroom with this note: "Much as we appreciate your service as the head of the school . . . you are still dearer to us because you are an upright, judicious, fearless and patriotic citizen whose example and influence is always present to raise us above sectional prejudice, and unite us in a broadminded endeavor to work for the good of the whole town."

In Helen Childs, Frank Boyden gained an inestimable helpmate, soulmate, and companion whose loyalty, ability, and character contributed immeasurably to his own personal happiness and professional success. Teacher, housekeeper, hostess, confidante, school mother, and spouse, Mrs. Boyden was her husband's equal in every aspect of school work. In fact, many Deerfield alumni contend she was the real genius behind the academy's success, the single most important influence on their young lives. As Michael Platt aptly suggests, "The marriage of Mr. and Mrs. Boyden was a long-lasting conspiracy for the good; their good, and the good of all they met. Its consequences were immense. They are still happening."

8

WORKING TOGETHER

Boyden had made an admirable beginning at Deerfield Academy and Dickinson High School, but the bulk of the work remained yet ahead. While most of Deerfield celebrated the school's revival, some townspeople remained indifferent. Undaunted, Boyden hitched up his horse-drawn buggy and took to Deerfield's dusty roads. Riding circuit in the hills to the west and the meadows to the south, Boyden recruited students, asked for favors, and campaigned for school support. Armed with a fierce conviction about the importance of education in an increasingly technical and materialistic society, the headmaster fought especially hard for children whose parents refused to abandon outdated notions of rural schooling.

"Away up on the hillside," Boyden recalled, "there was a family whose ancestors had fought at Bunker Hill. They had two splendid boys, and took them out of school in the spring of their sophomore year. We felt pretty strongly that they should be in school, so I went to see the father, and after we had talked about the weather and the prospect for the crops and various other things, we finally got down to the question of keeping the boys in school. He said, 'Mr. Boyden, I can not afford to do it.' I proposed that we send somebody to work for a month, and the boys themselves work early in the morning and after school, and after a good deal of argument, I finally persuaded him. The boys came back and graduated. The money came in for one of them to go to Worcester Tech and the other to go to the Lowell Textile School. Today they are strong men in their professions."

Girls in those days were often prejudiced by parental reluctance to educate them. On one occasion, when a girl withdrew from Deerfield and Dickinson to work in a telephone office, Boyden

immediately visited her father. "We sat around and talked for an
hour, and finally when it seemed to be the right moment, I said
'Sadie will be back to school tomorrow morning, won't she?'

"'What's the use,' he said, 'She will get married pretty soon.'

"Then I asked him, 'Does it make any difference what kind of man
she marries?'

"Well, he said he hadn't thought anything about that, and she came
back to school the next morning.

"She graduated and her matrimonial prospects are good."

Boyden responded to popular concerns about Deerfield Academy
and Dickinson High School's emphasis on impractical "book
learning" by developing a manual training program for boys and a
home economics course for girls. Two members of the Class of 1913
who lived across the river in West Deerfield remember first meeting
the headmaster. "He came to our home to see about a log to use in
Manual Training. People had to give everything in those days, there
was no money to buy anything. Also he came to West Deerfield to
plan about five children coming to Deerfield that year. He always
had to be busy. He reached into mother's work basket, took a spool
of thread, and wound and rewound all the while he was talking. We
knew his whole mind was on his school."

Boyden recruited seven scholars from those western hills and built
a raft for them to cross the river, which shortened their daily
commute by more than half. "Two boys pulled the raft with a heavy
wire until the river froze over. Two trips were made each way with
seven to transport. Later we had a team of horses to carry us in a
three seated wagon."

The Deerfield and Dickinson manual training program was a
popular and practical complement to the school's liberal arts
curriculum. A pragmatic way to provide amenities and make capital
improvements the school could not afford, it also gave the boys a
material stake in Deerfield and Dickinson that was one of the surest
ways to develop school loyalty.

"We don't make many coat hangers, and things like that," Boyden
said. "We make wheel-barrows and incubators, and things of really
practical use. And what is more, they work. We are flooded with
applications for them. We wanted lockers for our athletic teams, but

we did not have the money to buy the thousand feet of lumber we needed. One boy's father said he would give us the lumber standing if we would cut it. Another offered his team to haul it to the mill. And still another offered his to haul it home. One Saturday, sixteen of the big fellows decided they would go on the job, so we started with our team and eight cross cut saws. We met a lumberman who asked us what we were going to do. We told him, 'Cut a thousand feet of lumber.' He said, 'You can't do it today.' Well we struck the woods at 10:45. At 11:30 we had our thousand feet down and at 11:45 we had the first load on the wagon. Then we ate lunch, and piled up two or three cords of wood for the man who owned the wood, so he would be generous again some time. We got our thousand feet of lumber to the mill that night. All it cost us was $3.35 to get it delivered back again to Deerfield.

"At another time we wanted shower baths, but we did not have any money. Someone told us if we did all the manual labor, they would furnish the money. We did it, and we have shower baths. In the same way our building was wired for electrical lights. If they do things themselves, they appreciate them all the more. It arouses school spirit."

Although Boyden is sometimes criticized for favoring boys over girls, this criticism is unfounded in those early years when students were few and girls outnumbered boys. In fact, one member of the Class of 1912 believed Boyden was more partial to girls: "As long as the girls were industrious we boys thought at first that it would be all right to let them do the major part of the work of the class. But we were soon enlightened in that part by Mr. Boyden and made to understand that we eight boys were expected to work hard and make ourselves sufficient to offset the effect of twenty girls. This was no easy task either as the girls were really students and could keep ahead of the boys easily."

Boyden did enjoy a special bond with the boys based on their mutual interest in athletics. But he also cared for the girls by recruiting superior female teachers. Just as Deerfield and Dickinson boys considered the headmaster a role model, Deerfield and Dickinson girls revered eminent women faculty like C. Alice Baker, Minnie Hawks, and Helen Childs. Each afternoon, while the boys

worked or played sports with the headmaster, Boyden divided the girls "into four groups each in charge of one of four teachers. I do not lay particular value on the things they do, whether sewing or basketry, or what, but I want them thrown for an hour every afternoon with a woman of culture and refinement. When they talk together, play together, and walk together, it leaves a stamp upon them as nothing else can do."

Boyden, too, went to great lengths for Deerfield and Dickinson girls, as Mary Eddy '06 attests. "I have many pleasant memories of Mr. Boyden and the school, the schoolwork, the games, the plays in which we took part, sitting on the stairs at noon singing happy songs of that era. What fun we had. I remember the Alumni dinners cooked and served by mothers of the students. And the delicious homemade cake baked by the good women of the town. And through all our school days we knew the interest, kindness and friendship of Mr. Boyden."

After graduating from Deerfield and Dickinson, Mary Eddy planned to attend North Adams Normal School. "To me, North Adams seemed like the other side of the world. I had never spent a night away from my family and as September came nearer my heart was heavy with home sickness. At last the great day came and my mother and I took the trolley car to the Greenfield railroad station. Mr. Boyden came to see me off. As the train approached, my heart sank lower. My dear mother with tears in her eyes said to Mr. Boyden, 'I wish you were going with Mary.' He immediately said he would and over the hills and through the Hoosac Tunnel we went to school. Mr. Boyden presented me to some member of the faculty and life seemed a little brighter."

It was not long before word of Boyden's accomplishments spread beyond Deerfield. In 1908 the Boston *Globe* reported, "Frank L. Boyden, Principal of Deerfield Academy and Dickinson High School at Deerfield MA is doing such remarkable work that it has attracted the attention of the outside world. Mr. Boyden is solving some of the problems of a country town, not in theory but in practice." Under Boyden's leadership, Deerfield Academy and Dickinson High School clearly was on its way to longer-standing success.

9

TOM ASHLEY

Each year at commencement time, Deerfield's headmaster assembles the graduating class to tell the story of Tom Ashley '11. In Boyden's words, "He was without exception the finest boy we have ever had in our Academy. His life has been an inspiration." Lewis Perry, former headmaster of Phillips Exeter Academy and a dear Boyden friend, considered Ashley's life "a remarkably clear illustration of Mr. Boyden's philosophy of education."

Boyden's few notes on Ashley describe him as a "peculiar boy" with a "funny lisp" that contributed to his shy disposition. A handsome youth with a sturdy athletic frame that eventually stretched to six feet, four inches, Tom's New England roots ran deep. Tom's father, Charles Ashley, was an eighth-generation descendant of Deerfield's first settlers. Proprietor of one of the largest farms in the Pocumtuck Valley, Charles held many public offices, including assessor, selectman, chairman of the Franklin County draft board and state representative.

Charles Ashley understood the importance of proper schooling. A Deerfield alumnus himself, he sent Tom's older brother John to Deerfield and Amherst. Tom's sisters, Mildred and Natalie, likewise attended the academy before enrolling at Wellesley and the Conservatory of Music. But Charles had greater difficulty persuading Tom about the academy's merits.

Tom Ashley was not naturally inclined to book learning. After finishing his farm chores, Ashley preferred passing "his spare time in the nearby woodlands and streams." According to his brother, Ashley "enjoyed trapping and hunting and was a crack shot and an excellent swimmer." On one occasion his swimming ability saved a drowning companion. Ashley's own journals describe swimming "58

times in 1907," including a frigid plunge on 23 March when he "had
to wade through snow drifts to get to water." Ashley's other
accounts list the number of "snakes killed" and "game shot,"
including blue jays, red squirrels, muskrats, mudturtles, rats, crows,
doves, skunks, pigs, and cats. Ashley hunted for fun. He also
trapped for modest profit. His 1909 "trapping account of skunks and
animals" indicates the sale of a "first batch" from which he "got
$4.80."

Boyden first approached Ashley in 1907 about attending the
academy. According to Lewis Perry, "Tom grunted a refusal." But
Boyden persisted. He told Ashley's father to bring Tom to the
village post office before classes began on opening day. When the
two men and the boy met at the appointed time, the academy bell
rang announcing a new school day. At this point, Boyden said,
"There's the bell, Tom. Would you mind going up to school and
opening the door? Tell Miss Hawkes I will be there in a few
minutes."

A dutiful boy glad of something to do, Tom took the keys to
school and waited for Boyden as instructed. But Boyden was "by
chance" quite busy that morning and kept out of Tom's way. When
lunch hour arrived, Boyden asked Tom to stay. After lunch, he
invited Tom to play football with the academy boys later that
afternoon. "This was the one thing Tom would have been willing to
do," Perry said, "and from that afternoon he was a bona fide member
of Deerfield Academy."

For Ashley, who was not a brilliant student, Deerfield was a place
to have fun, be with friends, learn a few lessons, and play sports.
Tom's "Complete record of Athelectics (sic)" indicates the 1909
Deerfield and Dickinson football team boasted a 4-2 season, with
quarterback Boyden handing off to Ashley for seven of the team's
twenty-two touchdowns. The following year, with Ashley as captain,
Deerfield outscored opponents 126 to 18.

As good a gridder as Ashley was, he was even better at basketball.
Playing at home as a senior forward, Ashley outscored Henry Flynt's
entire Monson Academy squad in a 35-15 rout. Traveling to Monson
one month later, Flynt returned Ashley's favor by scoring twenty
points in a 48-16 Monson victory. Flynt later became instrumental

in Deerfield's history, both as chairman of the academy's board of trustees and inspiration for the town of Deerfield's historic preservation.

While Boyden believed basketball was the sport best suited for school-wide participation, no pastime was dearer to his heart than baseball. Since his appointment as Deerfield principal, Boyden had played first base and batted clean-up for the academy nine. In 1908, Ashley's first season, Boyden batted .222. The following spring, when Boyden's average dropped to .186, Ashley replaced him at clean-up.

Confident and able on Deerfield's athletic fields, Ashley was diffident and awkward off them. He approached his studies with stubborn determination. But like most schoolboys, he also enjoyed passing notes. Sitting in Boyden's physical geography class daydreaming of hunting and trapping, Tom drew pictures of skunks and passed them to a fair-haired female classmate seated across the aisle. This was not the only time Tom had skunks foremost in his thoughts. At school dances, Deerfield girls tried to engage Tom in conversation. Once while sitting with his assigned partner groping for something to say, Tom remarked, "Great night for skunks isn't it."

Under Boyden's direction, Ashley developed slowly and steadily. By commencement 1911, Ashley was confident enough to deliver a rendition of Henry Ward Beecher's "The Message of Our Flag." "You go to serve our country in the cause of liberty," he professed. "And if you fall in that struggle, may some kind hand wrap about you the flag of your country, and may you die with its sacred touch upon you."

Ashley's 1911 hunting license lists his occupation as "Farmer." Up to that point there is little indication he aspired to anything else. But Ashley's goals were changing. He decided to renew his Deerfield studies for another year. By the following summer Ashley's academic record was strong enough to earn him a place in Amherst College's class of 1916.

Ashley did not distinguish himself first in the Amherst classroom. Within days of school's opening, the football captain wrote Boyden describing Tom's early notoriety. "I heard of Ashley before he

entered College, and immediately looked him up In fact he's already well-known around college, owing to the prominent part he took in the Freshman-Sophomore Flag Rush," an annual sporting event comparable to the game of capture the flag.

Ashley's initiation to collegiate academics was more difficult. Schoolwork had never come easily for him and the challenge of Amherst coursework was compounded by President Meicklejohn's increasingly rigorous intellectual standards. In November, Ashley wrote Boyden, "There is practically no chance of my staying now, as the 12 weeks marks were even worse than the first six weeks It seems the more I study, the worse I get haven't done anything but eat, sleep, and study since Thanksgiving and the result seems pretty poor." Ashley completed the first semester with three C's, two D's, and a 69 average.

Boyden secured a tutor for Ashley as he did for many former Deerfield students having difficulty in their college years. But the extra help did little good. "We are just starting algebra," Ashley wrote Boyden, "they all say it is worse than trig so I am as well as canned in that course." Although Ashley never scored better than a D in math and dropped the subject after his sophomore year, he had greater success in the humanities and social sciences. Ashley's English grades were consistent B's, and his history scores were frequently A's.

Despite the football coach's prediction that he would be captain his senior year, Tom's introduction to Amherst athletics was little better than his early experience in the classroom. "We are going to have a bum freshman football team," he wrote, "as we haven't had eleven men out but one night so far this season I have been playing right half so far but can't do anything there as you know I am naturally a left-handed runner."

Boyden asked Ashley to coach Deerfield football that fall but Tom declined. He had too much work without further responsibilities and was "not looking for any official job as that isn't my line." In later years Ashley traveled more frequently down the valley to visit his mentor and friend and to assist in coaching both the football and basketball teams.

As a sophomore Ashley made the varsity football team as substitute halfback. The following year he moved to right tackle, where his blocking "bolstered the line to such an extent that Amherst had one of its most successful seasons," including a 31-0 rout of rival Williams College. Winter seasons Ashley helped revive basketball as an interscholastic sport. In spring Tom earned three baseball letters as an outfielder and catcher.

As a senior Ashley became increasingly interested in schoolmastering. During winter break he coached three Deerfield basketball practices, emphasizing the up-tempo pace, perimeter shooting, and aggressive rebounding that has characterized so many Deerfield quintets. "I have been trying to teach them . . . to pass or shoot quickly and generally coming back as fast as they can. It would seem best to lay a lot of stress on dribbling . . . and on following up on long shots." That spring Ashley requested a recommendation from Boyden for a "possible position at St. Mark's School in Southboro." But Boyden had other plans for Tom. He appointed Ashley to the Deerfield faculty instead.

By 1916 the Ashley-Boyden bond had developed to such a point that Boyden, while hospitalized at Boston's Peter Bent Brigham for an unspecified but critical illness, wrote Tom asking him to "leave an eye out for my boys . . . If I don't come out of this o.k." A young man of twenty-two, Ashley had already fulfilled the headmaster's "fondest hopes." "You have been and done the things I would have liked to do and be," wrote Boyden. "I hope for my boys the same kind of career." Although Boyden soon recovered, that letter turned up in Boyden's 1934 appointment book as testimony to Ashley's profound, enduring influence on the headmaster.

When Ashley joined the Deerfield faculty in 1916, Boyden was striving to develop an academy that would compare favorably with Andover and Exeter. Restoring the boarding department was an essential aspect of this plan. Boyden consequently renovated and expanded the John Williams House and installed Ashley as its first contemporary boarding schoolmaster.

Ashley understood the importance of marketing Boyden's ideas in a way the headmaster did not. For years Boyden had refused to publish a school catalogue because he believed the money was better

spent on scholarships and operating expenses. Ashley persuaded him otherwise. While studying educational psychology at Columbia University during the summer of 1916, Ashley suggested the academy prepare "a catalogue for advertising and for soliciting patrons."

Although Boyden had insisted he had no real "philosophy of education," Ashley explored specific aspects of the headmaster's implicit program in drafts of that first catalogue. Ashley's words are as good as any ever written about Boyden's approach to schooling:

"Believing that the welfare of the group is best attained thru the development of the individual; the chief aim of Deerfield Academy is the all around development of its individual students. A development not confined to the mind alone but to all phases of life closely related to the school and whose direction the school may properly undertake. Development that will enable the student to better take his place, and be of greater influence in that field of endeavor which may be chosen in after life, as well as among his fellows. In short, the development of the whole individual as a member of society.

This ideal involves intellectual development, a desire of service thru influence, and a high standard of character and physical development. Yet while courses in study and physical development can be taught as such, ethics can not be treated as a formal subject. All the means of encouraging a student to stand for the right things in life must be indirect. The personal element comes in. A system can not develop character. Here rules will not make good citizens. Therefore we believe that the individuality of the student should be preserved and directed, not crushed and forced to conform to a rigid system.

Thus our aim in the work of the school is to preserve the individuality of the student in question of influence thru the tone of the school. An underlying almost unconscious feeling that the school shall stand for the right things."

Ashley's career as Deerfield schoolmaster ended when the United States entered World War I in April 1917. Within a week of

President Woodrow Wilson's declaration of war, well before recruiting stations opened, Tom Ashley traveled to Boston to enlist. Mrs. Sheldon had tried unsuccessfully to persuade him to wait "till the need seemed more imperative." But "Tom made his choice," according to Professor Thompson, "while choice was still his to make."

Months before graduating from Amherst, Ashley had defended "The Position of Germany in World Politics" in his senior thesis. A year later, Ashley found himself in the Marine Corps preparing to kill Germans. "All they care about here is results, "Ashley wrote Boyden from Norfolk, Virginia, in May 1917, "That sort of system just suits me fine." Although the Marine Corps agreed with Tom, his father had doubts. As chairman of the local draft board, Charles Ashley had exhorted his boys to enlist. "I could not hold up my head if they had shown the yellow streak I run across every day in trying to do my duty and get soldiers for Camp Devens," he confided in a friend. But Charles feared for his youngest son. "I am afraid he will want to play the war game as he did football and it can't be done."

At Amherst Ashley had written, "It seems to me that life is not worth living without some definite object." At Quantico in 1918 Tom discovered that object on the eve of departure for combat. "You see I finally got what I have been trying to for the last ten months. I now have a definite goal to work for. Know just what kind of work I will have to do and where I am going and have a section of my own to make what I can out of Moreover the final destination of the company leaves nothing to be desired . . . It's surely a great relief not to be wondering all the time whether or not you will be shelved in Guam of China for the duration of the war."

War had turned Deerfield's former schoolboy and aspiring schoolmaster into an officer. "My practice at school teaching comes in very handy now," he wrote, "for I have to teach school an hour every day to a big class, not history or algebra, but on the latest and most scientific, methods of killing germans. Still the method of teaching both is about the same."

In February 1918, while Ashley's Second Division concluded preparation for European assignment, the Germans launched an offensive to occupy Paris before the Americans arrived in full force.

Capitalizing on March and April victories on the Sommes and in
Flanders, the Germans mustered 300,000 men for a May assault on
the French capital. On 27 May the fourteen German divisions broke
through Allied lines and advanced ten miles in a single day, the
biggest daily advance since the war began. By 1 June, when the 2d
Division joined the battle, the Germans had reached the Marne River
sixty miles east-northeast of Paris.

On 30 May Lieutenant Ashley was encamped at a staging area
west of Paris. At 4:00 a.m., 31 May, Ashley's division embarked for
Meaux. Beyond Meaux the road went straight to the front with
glimpses of the Marne over the soldiers' right shoulders. On 2 June,
according to Ashley's friend, Keller Rockey, "Our battalion formed
the advance guard . . . and went into position near Premont. This
was another hard day. The enemy were in sight and we were
expecting to attack." Ashley's company located and fortified
positions, brought up ammunitions and supplies, then were relieved
toward nightfall, suffering several casualties under heavy shell fire.

The next two days Ashley rested awaiting the coming fury. "We
were camped in a most delightful spot in a meadow sheltered from
the enemy artillery fire to an extent and in the shadow of a beautiful
French chateau," Rockey wrote Ashley's father. "The inhabitants had
left the country just a few days before, there were fresh vegetables
growing in the gardens, a cellar full of potatoes in the chateau,
rabbits and cattle." Awaiting further orders, Rockey and Ashley
"went up and wandered through the chateau which was an immense
and interesting old place." There in that meadow beside the Marne,
Ashley could not have helped but recall his Deerfield home.

Orders arrived and Ashley's company moved back into direct fire,
replacing the French who dropped back, tired out and outnumbered.
At 5:00 p.m., 5 June the Germans attacked. "Driving at Hill 165
from the North and Northeast they came out on a wonderfully
clear day, in two thin brown columns advancing in perfect order until
two thirds of the column, we judge, were in view. The rifle and
machine gun fire were incessant and overhead the shrapnel was
bursting. Then the shrapnel came on target at each shot. It broke
just over and just ahead of the columns and then the burst spread
over the very green in which we could see the column moving. The

white patches would roll away and we could see that some of the columns were still there, slowed up, and it seemed perfect suicide for them to try that. You couldn't begrudge a tribute to their pluck at that. Then under that deadly fire and the barrage of rifle and machine gun fire, the Boche stopped. It was too much for any men. They burrowed in or broke to the cover of woods and you could follow them by the ripples of green wheat as they raced over."

After turning the German attack, orders arrived for an Allied advance to "straighten out the lines and recover lost territory." According to Lieutenant R. M. Wilcox, Ashley's fellow officer and close companion, "Zero hour was to be 3:45 A.M. I got over to the 67th Company trenches in time to see Tom with his watch in hand counting the seconds until 3:45, his men watching him confidently. Our barrage had begun and the enemy was replying actively with his artillery but Tom stood there calmly and confidently, at times looking out beyond as though trying to see through the dim half-light which hid the enemy fully two hundred kilometers in the edge of the extremes. At 3:45, I heard him call to his men, 'Over You Go!' And every man sprang from the trench to follow him."

"We were crossing a wheat field," said Corporal Charles Murphy. "The Boche were hidden in little clumps of woods where they had planted nests of machine guns." According to Rockey, "It was mighty nasty going . . . The French on our left were held up early. The other battalion could not attack thru no fault of their own." Only Ashley's battalion went through and it paid dearly. "Exposed and subjected to severe machine gun fire from both flanks as well as heavy artillery and rifle fire from the front," the 67th suffered extreme casualties. But Ashley led his battalion, now comprised of fewer than twenty men, directly toward the enemy fire. "Come On Follow Me," Ashley cried as he "charged the Germans."

"If," Ashley wrote at Amherst, "he disregards death entirely and sets out to accomplish his object boldly and without any thought of being halted by the grim reaper . . . life is certainly worth living." At Chateau-Thierry, Ashley put this belief to a brutal test. He was cut down by a German machine gun, shot through the hips near sunrise 6 June 1918. "A super man in the fight," as described by an Amherst fraternity brother who fought by his side, Ashley died instantly. He

was buried where he fell, "in a wheat field where he stayed till the last."

Ashley's death amplified Boyden's resolve to fulfill the plan the two men once framed together. To a great extent, Boyden would build Deerfield Academy as a monument to Tom Ashley's exemplary spirit.

10

THE BOARDING DEPARTMENT

Boyden's interest in boarding students was consistent with his belief in the high school as an extended family. His commitment to educating children had always gone beyond the classroom. Like Charlie Garman, Boyden appreciated the wider implications of local effort. For both men, classroom teaching introduced issues of broader moral consciousness and civic duty. Although physically limited by their respective institutions, intellectually and spiritually Garman and Boyden shared a grand progressive vision for improving American life.

In 1913 Boyden traveled to Richmond, Virginia to address the American Playground Recreation Association. Boyden believed America was built by generations of hard-working, patriotic farm folk who had lived productive lives in country towns like Foxboro or Deerfield. Concerned about urbanization and industrialization that upset this Jeffersonian ideal, Boyden boldly suggested Deerfield Academy and Dickinson High School as a model for rural education reform nationwide.

"Ninety percent of the successful business men in Boston were born and brought up in the country," Boyden said. "If we are to continue to supply the cities with the men to conduct their business, we must put recreational work along the lines we have been discussing into their education. It seems to me a school which meets the physical, social, and moral needs of all the children of the whole community, a school which has turned out those who have become successful men and women, is the kind of school which should be put, as far as possible into every country community." Impressed by Boyden's words and accomplishments, the Playground Association, of which Theodore Roosevelt was a trustee, offered him a full-time

job. This appointment would have thrust Boyden immediately into national politics. Were it not for Howard "Joe" Gibbs, an Amherst classmate, fellow schoolmaster and founder of Eaglebrook School, Boyden might have accepted.

Gibbs first met Boyden in the fall of 1898 at Amherst where the two freshmen were familiarly known as "Joe" and "Bill." Both men came from modest socioeconomic backgrounds. Both worked after high school to save money for college tuition. Both were comparatively old for their class. Elected freshman vice president, Gibbs made a significant first impression. Boyden, on the other hand, saved his best for last. Gibbs and Boyden opted to teach after graduating in 1902. Gibbs became principal of the Worcester Academy Junior School, taught mathematics at Worcester Academy in 1909, accepted a year-long appointment as head of the Powder Point School in Duxbury, then moved once more to the Allen School in West Newton, which he ran until 1915.

Speaking perhaps as a man who had switched jobs too frequently, Gibbs counseled Boyden to reject the Recreation appointment. "I have thought a great deal about your suggestion of possibly changing your profession," he wrote in 1914. "The more I think of this the more surprised I am . . . You are the one man in the teaching profession whom I know intimately that I sincerely envy and of our entire class I have for some time thought you were the one doing the most worthy work and the most notable."

For an ambitious man in his mid-thirties the opportunity to leave a rural high school for national politics was tempting. But Boyden valued loyalty as Garman had done at Amherst. He declined the Recreation job and returned home with renewed conviction that his work as headmaster was personally significant and extrinsically vital for Deerfield and indirectly for America at large. With a taste of national recognition and growing self-confidence Boyden redoubled his efforts to build a great school.

At Richmond, Boyden had announced his school's local achievements to a national audience. When Boyden opened the Deerfield Academy and Dickinson High School boarding department in 1916, he planned on bringing youth from throughout the nation to Deerfield for a firsthand experience. Renovations were made to

accommodate resident students in the historic John Williams House. Tom Ashley was appointed Deerfield's first boarding schoolmaster.

Another reason compelled Boyden to open a boarding department. Although Deerfield Academy and Dickinson High School had won the 1904 battle to appropriate public money for a private school, the debate was again renewed with gloomier prospects for victory. To keep the school independent of public control, Boyden believed he had to increase its revenues and endowment. Enrolling tuition-paying boarding students from affluent families was an important step in this direction.

Since Boyden's 1904 contest with Bridges, the appropriations dispute had become a statewide concern, as rival parochial schools bickered over public funds. Amidst this bitter fight, the 1913 Massachusetts Supreme Court barely upheld the constitutionality of public aid for private education. In 1917 the state legislature proposed a constitutional amendment to settle this issue once and for all. This "anti-aid amendment" prohibited "public aid to any institution not owned and controlled by the public including any church or other religious authority." Plans for a state constitutional convention and subsequent fall referendum were adopted. Local communities were instructed to elect representative delegates.

Although Deerfield Academy and Dickinson High School was secular and nonparochial, it was a semiprivate school that depended on public funds. Without this money the school could not meet its operating expenses. Boyden consequently campaigned to represent Deerfield's opposition to the amendment at the convention. "I feel sure you can be elected without making promises of any kind whatever," Thomas Beard wrote Boyden. "All the people who know you have confidence in your ability and breadth of mind to be fair to the great body of the people rather than the so called interests who will have a strong influence on many delegates."

On 22 May 1917 Deerfield elected Boyden as its Republican delegate to the constitutional convention. Fresh from college, he had avoided taking a public position in the first appropriations battle. Now, older, more mature, ambitious, self-confident, and popularly respected, Boyden took the fight directly to the state legislature.

"A man must have a strategy as well as an ideal," Boyden said, "Only a fool fails to understand that." Realizing the odds for continued appropriation of public funds were slim, Boyden initiated plans for the boarding department as an alternate independent source of income. According to this strategy, tuition and board paid by resident students would net revenue to replace the anticipated loss of public funds.

At the convention, Boyden's ambitions were tempered by his lack of political experience. "I was very green to go down among those politicians," he remembered. "I didn't know what was up." Boyden's lobbying against the amendment failed. "Standing on the impregnable ground that public money should be spent on public purposes," the *New York Times* reported, "the Convention adopted the anti-aid amendment by a vote of 275 to 25." On 6 November a statewide majority exceeding 75,000 votes approved the amendment. All religious denominations would now have "a chance of peace with one another since the State will give them no money to squabble over."

Although a political novice at the time, Boyden was a veteran at winning friends and courting favors. He had lost the amendment fight but did make valuable acquaintances, most notably John McCormack, who would help Boyden in later years as a U.S. congressman and Speaker of the House. Almost fifty years after first meeting the headmaster McCormack recalled, "Many years ago in my first public office, I served with Frank Boyden in the Massachusetts Constitutional Convention of 1917-18. He is truly one of God's noblemen, a man dedicated to God, Mankind and to Country."

Ratifying the anti-aid amendment was one thing, enforcing it was another. While public funds to parochial schools were immediately terminated, Massachusetts temporarily permitted money voted to nonsectarian academies. Boyden consequently gained the time necessary to engineer Deerfield Academy's independence from public control.

Boyden turned immediately to Joe Gibbs for help. Since declining the Recreation job, Boyden had taken an active interest in Gibbs's work. The two men and their wives also shared an avid interest in Amherst football. "Thank you for your continued interest in this

little school," Gibbs wrote, "and thank you for the invitation to spend Sunday with you after the Amherst-Williams Game . . . we want to see you both and I am always hungry for good talks with you on people and the profession." On another occasion Gibbs added, "I never leave the phone from a talk with you without I am minded of many things I wanted to ask your advice about."

Although Gibbs urged Boyden to stay at Deerfield, he continued to pursue more mobile plans himself. In 1915 Gibbs quit teaching and opened a placement agency for parents seeking appropriate preparatory schools for their children. An able salesman, Gibbs pitched his services, "Only one who knows schools thoroughly and one whose interest is not bound to one school can understand and justly evaluate these subtle and important differences; and only one who knows and understands boys through years of intimate living with them can be reasonably sure to recommend the right school to the right boy."

Gibbs began to recommend students to Boyden at a time when Deerfield Academy and Dickinson High School badly needed them. In the fall of 1916 Boyden opened the boarding department. He now had to recruit students to fill those dormitory beds. "If there is any little service I can do for you," Gibbs wrote Boyden, "just *sic me on* to any one of your ultra conservatives." Selling the novel idea of boarding schools at this time when it was all but unheard of was a great challenge. Gibbs emphasized Boyden's conviction that schoolboys must be kept busy. "We grow weary when idle," Gibbs wrote, "because others being busy, we want company."

Gibbs and Boyden both suffered grave personal losses in 1918. Gibbs's wife died in February, and Tom Ashley fell before Prussian machine guns in June. That fall Gibbs abandoned his placement agency and joined the Deerfield faculty. For the bereaved Gibbs, Deerfield became a supportive place to reorient himself in the company of a dear friend. For Boyden, Gibbs sustained the thrust behind the boarding department Ashley had inaugurated. Years later Boyden wrote Gibbs's cousin, Mrs. Ernest Breed, "I could never begin to tell you how grateful I have always been for the advice and help which he generously gave when we were re-establishing Deerfield Academy as a boarding school. I had absolutely no

experience in that field of work, and without his tactful and understanding guidance could never have succeeded."

Drawing on his consulting experience and advertising acumen, Gibbs prepared Deerfield Academy and Dickinson High School's first published catalogue. This 1919 *Book of Views* was essential for Boyden's campaign to raise the $150,000 needed to purchase the public share of Deerfield Academy and Dickinson High School and reincorporate the school as a wholly private institution.

11

A PREP SCHOOL

The 1919 Deerfield *Book of Views* reflects a dramatic shift in Boyden's educational vision. References to Dickinson High School are notably absent. Henceforth, Boyden's school would be known, at least unofficially, as Deerfield Academy. Gone, too, were explicit emphases on rural education. Boyden's academy now advertised a "college preparatory" curriculum instead. Once a self-described country day school, Deerfield Academy and Dickinson High School hoped to join the prep school ranks. "It is on the approved list of the New England College Board and all colleges that admit without entrance examinations."

But Boyden's insistence on a well-rounded education endured. "A boy can not become weary or lonesome at Deerfield. Every hour not taken by schoolwork is filled with athletic rivalries, with football, basketball, baseball, and tennis; with swimming, mountain climbing, and weekend camping parties in the spring and fall; with skating, tobogganing, snowshoeing, and skiing in the winter; with debating, music, and dramatics; and there are occasional Saturday evening dances and at all times and in all seasons there is the companionship with fine fellows of the sort to make lifelong friends."

Boyden's plan for a nationally recognized college preparatory school required improved physical facilities. The *Book of Views* consequently includes a handsome elevation of Boyden Hall, a projected new dormitory named in a rare immodest moment for the headmaster. Plans also were on the drawing board for a new gymnasium. These new buildings represented a hefty capital investment Deerfield Academy and Dickinson High School could ill afford. The projected cost of the dormitory alone exceeded the school's total assets in 1919. But Boyden remained undaunted. He

intended to raise as much money as he could and borrow the rest.
Boyden had self-confidence and little fear of indebtedness, as another
favorite story, a mock letter written by a Brooklyn farmer to a New
Jersey tax collector, suggests:

"Dear Sir, I got your letter about what I owe. Now be patient. I
ain't forgot you. When I have the money I will pay you. But if this
was the first Judgment Day and you was no more prepared to meet
your Maker than I am to meet your account, you would sure go to
hell Trusting you will do this, I remain Sincerely yours."

With a net worth of $59,000 and only $2,000 subscribed for a
dormitory that cost more than $70,000, the Deerfield Academy and
Dickinson high school building program depended on Boyden's
unproven ability to raise money. But credit was the quickest way to
finance construction. Using the school's property as collateral,
Boyden borrowed $100,000.

By the winter of 1919, local fundraising prospects were exhausted
and the actual cost of constructing the dormitory exceeded the
budgeted sum. It was clear Boyden had to take a new approach. He
decided to visit Phillips Exeter Academy, where he hoped to gain
some helpful advice and perhaps cultivate a lucrative association.

Lewis Perry was principal of Exeter at this time. "Lewis combined
the finest attributes of a headmaster, a scholar, a teacher, a sportsman,
a gentleman, a friend," Boyden said. "He stood for quality, for old
verities which are sometimes compromised today, but which men of
conscience have always valued and respected. Perhaps his genius as
an administrator is best summed by saying that nothing was too large
or too small for him to accomplish; and that his accomplishments
were always achieved with tact and finesse ... Many of my own ideas
it is fair to say are only his re-dressed."

Perry was born on 3 January 1877. The son of a Williams College
professor, he attended Lawrenceville and Williams, where he was a
nationally ranked tennis player and captained the varsity baseball
team. After college Perry worked at several secondary schools before
returning to Williamstown to teach English literature.

Like Boyden, Perry was an unimpressive looking fellow. As one story put it: "In the 1920s Dr. Perry picked up three hitchhikers on his way from Exeter to Boston. The riders took turns guessing his occupation. One thought him a travelling salesman. The second suggested he was a veterinarian. The third pronounced him a bootlegger because 'your car is big, you're alone, and you seem to know a great many people on the road.'" The *New York Times* reported that these guesses pleased Perry because "despite his tweediness, he had not been identified as an educator. For Perry took pride in his informality, his democratic ways, and in his belief that a schoolmaster should not be a person apart from the common people."

When Perry accepted the Exeter headmaster appointment, the academy was rich in tradition but very short on cash. "That was in August 1914," one scribe wrote. "A world war had just begun, and the school though venerable and of a distinguished history had a heavy deficit." The *New York Times* estimated this debt at $250,000. When he retired in 1946, Exeter's endowment totaled $10 million, "much of it traceable to Perry's talent for getting considerably wealthy men to part with their money." This perhaps is why the Exeter principal was sympathetic to Deerfield's fiscal plight when Boyden arrived unannounced on that cold December day in 1919.

Perry remembers meeting Boyden on the last school day before Christmas break. "It had been a hard winter with more sickness than usual," Lewis Perry recalled. "Mrs. Perry asked me at breakfast what I was going to do that day. 'I shall dismiss the school, clear my desk, and then sleep for fourteen hours,' I replied. Only the first part of the program was successfully carried out. About eleven o'clock a stranger came into my office, a short, energetic man with what seemed to be particularly large glasses. Of all things, he carried under his arm pictures of school buildings and schoolboys. Now I was not immediately very much excited. But we sat down, and Frank Boyden began to talk about Deerfield. For the first time I heard the story of Tom Ashley. For the first time I realized what a private school could do for a community. For the first time I felt excitement about this school in the Deerfield Valley. Finally Mr. Boyden said, 'I hope I'm not keeping you from your lunch.' 'Oh

no,' I said, 'It's not nearly lunch time yet.' But when I looked at my watch, I found that it was quarter to three."

Boyden's meeting with Perry marked the beginning of a lifelong association between dear friends and their respective academies. "Lewis enriched hundreds of lives, both by the example of his own and by the direct assistance he was always generously willing to give," Boyden said. "I can not estimate how much my own life would have been diminished had it not been my privilege to know him." Boyden frequently relied on Perry's counsel. Perry gladly reciprocated, serving some thirty years as a Deerfield trustee.

Following this meeting with Perry, Boyden began to develop Deerfield's reputation as a school where students dismissed from rival institutions such as Exeter might save face and begin anew. Deerfield soon became known as a place where students who made a serious disciplinary mistake or two could return to learn from it. Under Boyden expulsion was nearly impossible, in part because there were few formal rules to break. "If you make a lot of rules, they never hit the fellow for whom you made the rule," Boyden said. "Two hours after making a rule you may want to change it." Although he revered President Lincoln, Boyden also admired Confederate General Robert E. Lee, who became a college president after surrendering at Appomatox. "A Boy," said Boyden quoting Lee, "is more important than any Rule."

There were several reasons for such disciplinary flexibility. Philosophically, Boyden had great confidence in man's inherent goodness. This was a significant departure from the stark, neopuritan disposition of many of his contemporaries. Pragmatically, a hard-line approach would have been self-defeating in a school that badly needed students. Disciplinary flexibility was crucial in those years when Boyden hoped to establish Deerfield among the ranks of New England prep schools.

Always striving to cultivate associations with other secondary schools, Boyden realized the role his school could play for students who were unqualified for admission or failed to make the grade at other academies. Dismissing a student was perhaps the most difficult task a headmaster faced. But the task would be far less disheartening if the "problem" student could be successfully referred to Boyden.

Likewise, prospective students who lacked the academic ability required for admission to Exeter, Andover, or St. Paul's might find Deerfield a worthy fallback school.

There is a misconception greatly exaggerated in Deerfield lore that these students referred by other academies were incorrigible malcontents and hard-nosed troublemakers. This clearly was not the case. Most students were recommended to Boyden because of academic difficulties associated with laziness or poor study habits, rather than low aptitude or mischievous behavior.

One of Deerfield's first "second chance" students, a Tennessee boy referred by Lewis Perry shortly after Boyden's visit to Exeter, is a representative example. "I think he is one of the most difficult boys that I have ever had," Boyden wrote, "not because of any real wrong with him morally or mentally, but because of a very superficial attitude toward his scholastic work and things worthwhile." This boy's principal failing at Exeter was scoring a 37 in physics and a 61 in history. At Deerfield, Boyden succeeded in preparing him for Dartmouth. "I felt that it was not so much a problem of getting him into Dartmouth, although he has a good deal of work to do, as to develop in him the right attitude toward scholarly attainments, and to put him in the frame of mind that will make him do for his own wishes good work after he got to college."

Perry referred another boy to Boyden whose principal difficulty at Exeter was his Jewish faith. In 1921 Perry's assistant, George Rogers, wrote Boyden, "One of our students . . . the son of a Jewish rabbi in Denver was required to withdraw from the Academy at the end of the fall. He is slow and diffident and seems to lack somewhat in physical and mental vigor. He was always diligent and attentive and I had the feeling he was giving his best. I suppose his diffidence and slowness touched my heart." Since Deerfield was less sectarian than Exeter, this boy not surprisingly thrived in an environment where he was less an outsider. His self-confidence restored, he scored all A's and high B's at Deerfield and matriculated at Harvard.

As Boyden salvaged Exeter discards, his reputation grew. "Your name and work have been so often mentioned in Exeter with warm praise," George Rogers wrote. Perry soon introduced Boyden to his colleague at Andover, Al Stearns, who referred the son of an

Amherst College professor. Although incapable of making the Andover grade, this boy enrolled at Deerfield and was "good enough" to become the 1923 class president.

While Exeter and Andover recommended students for academic reasons, Choate sent one for disciplinary reasons. "I should say that he was a boy above average in intelligence," C. Wardell St. John wrote Boyden, "but without sufficient seriousness of purpose to insure success in his work. Immediately following one foolish escapade with two other boys, he became involved in another concerning the perverted use of pumpkin pie as a missile. Otherwise he has been a likeable and respected member of our school." This boy thrived at Deerfield and later became president of Amherst's freshman class. Tragically, he died in a 1924 automobile accident. To this day, one of the most coveted prizes awarded each year at Deerfield's commencement is given in his memory to "the student in the graduating class who has done the most to promote the general happiness and joy of school life."

By 1921 Boyden had established an effective means both of filling his school's fledgling boarding department and advancing its reputation as a college preparatory school. By accepting students rejected by more established institutions, he not only won the confidence and appreciation of his fellow headmasters but also endeared himself to the students who were grateful for a second chance and eager to make it good.

12

SALESMANSHIP

Boyden always had been concerned about his school's public image. After borrowing $100,000 to finance the academy's ambitious building program, he pursued an even more aggressive strategy for "selling" Deerfield. Courtesy to visitors was top on the headmaster's expectations for students. "Losses do not often run into the millions for lack of courtesy," Boyden said,"but many concerns lose profitable business because they fail to show elementary consideration and kindness."

One Boyden apocryphal talk about courtesy described an unimpressive looking couple who visited the president of Harvard University. "You will have to be brief," the president said tartly. "I'm a very busy man and can give you only a few minutes." Not wishing to impose on such an important person, the husband and wife got up and left. They had intended to give Harvard millions of dollars, but they gave it instead to start a new university in the West. It was named for the donor, Leland Stanford.

The April 1921 *Pocumtuck*, the first Deerfield Academy and Dickinson High School newspaper, highlighted Boyden's emphasis on courtesy. "One of the great ways in which we can uphold the traditions and high standard of the school is in the matter of courtesy to strangers. Hundreds of people come to Deerfield every spring and most of them wish to look over our buildings. We must, therefore, be here and show them every courtesy in our power. We all of us want to maintain the high standard which has up to now been set in this respect, and this spring is the time when we should take particular pains."

The academy's physical appearance was equally important to Boyden, who carried a jackknife to unearth meddlesome weeds that

encroached on the school's footpaths. No school is more meticulously manicured than Deerfield. "You go to Exeter," said one prep school aficionado, "and you'll find fingerprints on the walls and toe scuffs on the stair risers. But not at Deerfield. The floors of the school building are waxed daily." Boyden himself professed, "If you keep floors of buildings and walls clean, it's like having your shoes shined and a clean shirt on."

Boyden found litter especially annoying, "There is always a tendency, especially in young people, to adopt a sort of careless attitude toward the property and affairs of others. One often notices around the buildings or grounds a scrap of paper, an old package, or something of the kind which has been accidentally left or dropped. We can not expect that there will be someone who does nothing but go around and pick up odd scraps which we happen to drop. So when you see a scrap of paper or anything else out of place even though it may not be your immediate concern, why not just pick it up and throw it in the nearest wastebasket."

Courtesy to strangers and well-groomed grounds were effective but passive means of selling the school. Boyden needed a more active instrument for getting Deerfield positive exposure. Athletics remained the most effective means to this end. Where Deerfield Academy and Dickinson High School once competed against local public high schools, it now scheduled games with New England's most respected prep schools.

In fall of 1921 Boyden asked the Choate headmaster, Rev. George St. John, "If it were possible for our athletic teams to meet in baseball or basketball I wish it might be arranged, as I am anxious to have our boys know the type of fellows who are in your school." In fact, Boyden was equally anxious for Choate boys to meet Deerfield boys. When the two schools' basketball squads first met on 14 February 1922, St. John was impressed. "And I may say further," he wrote Boyden, "that for every reason of splendid clean sportsmanship and mutual spirit of friendliness, we have never had any team here at Choate with whom our boys have enjoyed playing more than the one from Deerfield." This game marked the beginning of Deerfield's fierce rivalry with Choate.

That same winter, Boyden also scheduled a game with Loomis. "Our basketball team defeated Loomis Institute 36 to 18 Saturday at Windsor," Boyden wrote Bob Maynard. "They have a very wonderful school of the same class as Middlesex with a very dominant Harvard personality and tone. I think we have all of the finer things which they have without quite so much camouflage, but they really are fine people."

If Loomis prepared students for Harvard, Deerfield leaned toward Amherst. The 1921 commencement *Pocumtuck* boasted "Special attention is given to boys preparing for Amherst." Eight boys from Deerfield's graduating class were bound for Boyden's alma mater, the largest group entering Amherst from any prep school that year. Boyden hoped this growing Amherst connection would help resolve the academy's fiscal dilemma.

In 1921 Amherst was in the midst of a multimillion dollar centennial anniversary campaign. Boyden's classmate, Tug Wilson, an AT&T vice president, was Chairman of the fund drive. Bruce Barton, Boyden's boyhood friend, wrote the campaign announcement. Barton was born in 1886 in rural Tennessee. Like Boyden, Barton maintained a strong but unexacting Christian faith later popularized in *The Man Nobody Knows*, a best-selling novel describing Jesus as the perfect businessman. "He would be a national advertiser today, I am sure," Barton wrote. "He was the greatest advertiser of his day."

Valedictorian of the Amherst Class of 1907, Barton was voted the one who "gives greatest promise of success in life." After abandoning plans for graduate study, Barton moved to New York, where he worked for *Collier's Weekly*, supervised door-to-door book salesmen, and wrote an advertisement for *Harvard Classics*, a series designed to make a Harvard education accessible to every American. Barton next wrote copy that Norman Rockwell illustrated for Edison light bulbs. Barton's career breakthrough occurred in 1918, when he coined the slogan, "A man may be down; but he is never out," for a campaign benefiting the Salvation Army, YMCA, and YWCA that raised $200 million in one week. The following year, Barton joined Alex Osborn, a Buffalo adman, and Roy Durstine, a New York

journalist, to incorporate America's most celebrated advertising agency Batten, Barton, Durstine and Osborn.

In 1920 Barton published *The Gift of Amherst's Sons To Their Alma Mater On Her 100th Birthday 1921.* "A college is not buildings nor campus, but men," Barton wrote. "Many of the details of your own college experience have faded out of the picture; but large in the foreground loom the figures of the men who stimulated you to independent thinking, and left the impress of their character on yours. They were Amherst College to you A college is a man factory and must be judged by the character of the men it makes."

Barton's pamphlet agreed with Boyden's recollections of Amherst and his aspirations for Deerfield. Within weeks of receiving the announcement, the headmaster asked Barton for his assistance:

"Sometime I want to talk to you about our needs here, because they are very pressing. I feel sure that Amherst needs a school in which boys will be steered toward the college rather than away from it. That school must have sufficient social standing to warrant the best of our alumni sending their sons there. The types of boys whom we are sending to Amherst, most of whom would not have gone had they not come here, is sufficient excuse for our existence. Two weeks ago Mrs. George Pratt came here with her son, and asked us to finish preparing him for Harvard. I told her that I was not interested in preparing him for Harvard but that I would put him into Amherst next September. The boy was not interested in the Latin requirements nor in Amherst to any great extent, but he finally agreed to try and meet the requirements at Amherst, and as a result of the day at the Amherst and Williams game, is now an enthusiastic Amherst man. We send down this year 7 boys and I am sure they will prove an addition to the college mentally and athletically. Somehow we have arrived in a moment and I have hardly caught my breath yet. President Sills of Bowdoin wrote asking us to take the son of an intimate friend of his who needed some special work before entering Bowdoin. President Pennypacker, who is head of the Harvard Admission Board, has sent us 8 or 10 boys. Dr. Perry of Exeter has also been most kind in sending us boys whom he is

unable to take. We really seem to be established, but I do not see how we can even finish the year unless we have some strong financial assistance or promise of it before long. In addition to the Amherst end which I have described, Deerfield belongs to the whole country and if our school should close up, one of the great forces of preserving it as a typical New England village for the pleasure of thousands of tourists every summer, would be removed. Also the work we have been able to do along lines of rural education would receive a severe blow."

The Amherst Centennial Campaign raised $ 3 million. Deerfield's fiscal needs paled by comparison. With men like Barton, Wilson, and Maynard exhorting Amherst alumni, Boyden believed he could raise the $200,000 needed to purchase the public share of Deerfield Academy and Dickinson High School and finance an independent academy.

13

OBSTACLES

Boyden's plans for a nationally recognized prep school were not shared by everyone. Several Deerfield natives resented the headmaster's bid to seize control of their country day school. By 1923 Deerfield Academy and Dickinson High School was hurtling toward a critical juncture in its history. Friends of the school split into hostile factions. One group backed Boyden's plans for a private academy. The other fought to honor the Dickinson bequest strictly as a public high school.

The anti-Boyden coalition was comprised of those philosophically opposed to Boyden's plan and those personally at odds with the headmaster himself. In a persuasive editorial in the Greenfield *Recorder*, E. L. Coleman argued against the academy. "Can't you hear the children crying? Will not some friend of the children let their cry be heard; that their future may be assured and not be left subject to the invitation of the principal or a group of trustees who may not be interested in the rights of the boys and girls for whose benefit the Dickinson land and funds were given?"

Anti-Boyden sentiment was often expressed more vehemently, as in this editorial the headmaster managed to suppress before publication:

> A Fox from Foxboro came to town.
> He exploited our schools to his own renown.
> The name of Dickinson he quite forgot,
> Though this was only part of his plot.
> The best laid schemes of foxes and men
> Often go wrong in spite of them.
> Such is the case of Mr. How Do You Do,

He bit off more than he could chew.
Looking about him from his smug abode,
Coveted both sides of Albany Road.
The Ten Commandments he forgot,
And those words of Moses, "Thou shalt not."
From this said cause, later sermons be taught.
And when one feels inclined to steal,
An outraged public may appeal
To a higher court of last resort
Where crafty crooks get their desserts.
Where right is right, wrong is wrong,
Thus ends the burden of my song.

The anti-Boyden faction was understandably angry. For twenty years Deerfield citizens had supported the school's revival. Now Boyden's growing preference for boarders over day students and boys over girls suggested betrayal. Boyden was also building his academy at considerable public expense. Two thirds of the school's net worth was derived from the Dickinson bequest. Fifteen thousand dollars in annual operating expenses were underwritten by town appropriations. And the money Boyden raised for the new dormitory was borrowed against property deeded indirectly to the townspeople.

According to Elizabeth Pratt Whitman, an alumna and mother of two Deerfield and Dickinson students, "The Trustees have in the last years run the school into a $100,000 debt to build dormitories. Or to put it plainly, they have impoverished the Dickinson High School for the sake of establishing a boys' boarding school. We are told that there are rich philanthropists who are willing to put huge sums into the new private school only under the condition that our village gives up its birthright. When philanthropy and wealth go together, isn't it a pity they have to exploit a little village like Deerfield. Why not go to a town that has no established school? We resent being asked to give up the center of our old street to rich men for a private school for city boys."

Although dispute over control of the school was the principal point in this debate, maintenance of the town library was a divisive secondary issue. In addition to her interest in the high school, Esther

Dickinson had allotted money for a public library and reading room. When the Dickinson School Building was constructed in 1878, its north wing was explicitly reserved for this purpose. But Boyden converted the library to classrooms as the boarding department expanded and enrollment grew.

Harriet Childs argued for restoration of the Dickinson Library, "When the trustees insisted that the library could no longer be permitted where it was, where were the books taken? Come with me and I will show you. Up a side street, across a weed-grown yard, where the grass is never cut, we make our way to the shabby Town Hall building. After carefully stepping over broken slates from the roof, we pass down an ill smelling corridor into a dismantled school room. We look in vain for any hint as to how the room is to be heated during the coming winter."

Indignant about Boyden's neglect of the library, Childs also held a personal grudge. Childs graduated from Deerfield and Dickinson in 1903, Boyden's first year as principal. After studying at Smith, she taught German, English, and American history at high schools in Vermont, New York, and Connecticut, where she strived to emulate Boyden as an all-around schoolteacher. "My principal told me last June that the senior essays were the best that he had received and that he credited the feat to their English teacher," Childs wrote Boyden. "I am coaching three teams in basketball and expect to begin folk dancing this winter. I have had the entire responsibility of coaching school plays ever since I came and they have been very successful."

In 1914 Childs asked Boyden for a teaching job at Deerfield and Dickinson. As part of her query, she offered suggestions for upgrading the education afforded Deerfield girls. "I thought that just as you have engraved on cups the names of the boys who do all around good work, each girl who did good work in school, in the homemaker course, in physical work as shown by her interest in teams, and in her observation of laws of hygiene might be given a kind of emblem of her study in something to wear, for example, a crystal heart pendant. They're not expensive and might symbolize cleanliness of thought, action and purpose." Boyden declined Childs petition. Although she later served twenty-eight years as dean for

girls at Greenfield High School, Childs may have never fully accepted Boyden's rejection.

Harriet Childs was not the only one angered by Boyden's neglect of the library. With the reading room closed and the books stored in the abandoned town hall, Mrs. Flower, the Dickinson librarian, lost her job. Rallying to his wife's defense, Harold Flower became Boyden's most vehement opponent. Flower was among a small, vocal group that included Philip Ball and Winthrop Arms who wanted complete public control of Deerfield Academy and Dickinson High School. Flower advocated the town seize the school's property by eminent domain, then lease or sell it back to the academy trustees. In so doing, the town would cease underwriting Boyden's privatization of the semipublic institution. The income from this sale could then be applied toward construction of a new public high school in South Deerfield where most students now lived.

Boyden, on the other hand, hoped to purchase the town's interest in Deerfield and Dickinson at a fair market valuation. The town would then receive its share of the Dickinson funds and Boyden could run his school without further public interference. This plan hinged on Boyden's ability to raise the funds needed to finance the buy-out. But Boyden exaggerated Amherst alumni interest in his academy. Giving money to a one-hundred-year-old college was quite different from contributing to a prep school threatened by eminent domain. Even the most enthusiastic Deerfield Academy supporters had reservations about underwriting Boyden's enterprise.

One of the headmaster's biggest fund-raising obstacles was the extent the academy was identified exclusively with his own work. If Deerfield Academy was the lengthened shadow of a great man, what would happen in Boyden's absence? Few men would be sufficiently able and willing to succeed Boyden as headmaster of a school with an antiquated physical plant and sizeable debt.

After meeting with a prospective donor who later became president of Deerfield's board of trustees, Boyden wrote, "Mr. Plunkett's objection to the school is that it is a one man institution; that if I were to die or should find it necessary to leave, it would be difficult to get anyone to come in and carry on the work successfully." Bob Maynard concurred. "It is extremely necessary that we build an

organization to make the school independent of either you or me or anybody else, so as to have a proposition on which we could go to people for money."

Phenomenal as Boyden's achievement was, it made little sense to contribute to a school whose longer-term prospects seemed dubious. But no worthy Boyden successor would be found until the academy's fiscal foundation was significantly improved. This is one reason Boyden felt obliged to remain at Deerfield as long as he did. "Without being conceited," Boyden wrote, "I must admit that this is probably true, for our equipment is not sufficient to attract the type of man whom we should want."

In 1922 Deerfield's physical plant was woefully inadequate for a college preparatory academy. The original Dickinson school building was within years of official condemnation. "It has never been repaired since its erection," Boyden wrote. "It was always unsatisfactory and now we are able to use it only under the greatest difficulties." More problematic, the number of dormitory beds was far fewer than those required to accommodate the boarding students necessary for Deerfield to remain solvent. "This would involve another dormitory," Boyden wrote, "and that in turn, an enlargement of the dining hall." Then there was the question of a new fieldhouse. As strong an emphasis as Boyden placed on athletics, Deerfield lacked a gymnasium altogether. For years it had avoided this cost by converting a second floor study hall into a basketball floor each afternoon. Deerfield clearly could not charge a $1,000 tuition with such modest facilities.

Although Boyden might purchase the town's share of Deerfield Academy and Dickinson High School for $150,000, securing the academy's fiscal independence meant little if the academy could not attract enough boarding scholars to pay its bills. Maynard figured the school had to raise nearly $500,000 to become completely self-supporting. This sum would defray the cost of a new dormitory, gymnasium, and recitation hall, as well as an addition to the dining hall.

Raising money to finance the Deerfield and Dickinson buy-out was one obstacle, securing legislative approval for this purchase was another. Since Deerfield Academy and Dickinson High School was

officially incorporated by an act of the Massachusetts state legislature, the legislature retained sole authority to dissolve it. Until he established the probability of such approval, Boyden's prospects for raising money were slim. In January 1922 Maynard wrote Boyden, "I hope you can push that legal investigation because without that I can not see how we can have a solid foundation of fact on which to build the organization."

Boyden was no stranger to the law. His experience at the constitutional convention had provided a firsthand lesson in legislative politics. As a convention delegate, Boyden had introduced an amendment permitting towns that did not have a public high school to contribute to private schools willing to educate local children free of charge. Although this amendment was defeated, Boyden said, "Our town counsel felt that it would be perfectly legal for us to get around the issue by making an appropriation for the tuition of the high school pupils rather than a direct appropriation to the Academy."

By redefining the town's annual appropriation as a tuition subsidy for each pupil rather than an outright grant to the school, Deerfield Academy and Dickinson High School effectively circumvented the law until it was challenged again in 1922. Soon after the 1917 convention ended, Boyden and his friend John Haigis, the owner of the Greenfield *Gazette* later elected state treasurer, began to read law with Frederick L. Greene. While Deerfield Academy legend maintains Boyden was considering leaving education to practice law at this time, it is more likely the headmaster knew his school faced complicated litigation. Boyden wanted to understand the law firsthand. Too much was at stake in this case for him to delegate complete power of attorney.

In the summer of 1922 the legal loophole allowing Deerfield and Dickinson to receive public money through individual tuition subsidies closed. When the Boston School Committee proposed paying tuition for teachers studying at Boston University and Boston College, the anti-aid issue reappeared. Payson Smith, the commissioner of education, promptly notified all private schools, Deerfield and Dickinson included, that public appropriations for tuition were no longer permissible. Smith also terminated Deerfield's

exemption from a law requiring towns with five hundred householders or more to maintain a public high school. He instructed Deerfield to convert Deerfield Academy and Dickinson High School to a wholly public high school by 1 July 1923 or complete construction of a new high school no later than 1 January 1924.

Boyden's initial reaction to Smith's pronouncement was a rare expression of despair. "I am quite reconciled to have done what I have been permitted to do during the last twenty years and start something else," he wrote Maynard, "but it is such an undertaking to build an educational institution to the position which ours occupies and there are so few good schools in existence." Never one to give up easily, Boyden prepared for a conclusive effort. "I do not in any way intend to give up the ship until the very last gun is fired."

14

DEALMAKING

With his life's work at stake and the distinct possibility of future failure, Frank Boyden rededicated himself to working as he had never worked before. But unlike those first days at Deerfield, when he labored alone, Boyden now had the advantage of many well-connected friends. Together with classmates Bob Maynard, Tug Wilson, Bob Cleeland, and Wilmot Trevoy, the headmaster canvassed Amherst alumni for generous donors.

Before long, Boyden's efforts began to pay dividends. Amherst College President Alexander Meicklejohn endorsed the academy: "The work of the school is so important and the urgency of the situation so great that I wish a committee might be formed to make plans for dealing with the Deerfield situation as the Centennial Gift Committee did with the College situation."

Calvin Coolidge, vice president of the United States and an Amherst alumnus (1895) offered his support: "It is with real regret that I have heard that there is a possibility of the closing of Deerfield Academy. Mr. Boyden has built up a remarkable school for the development of character, as well as the mind, and I think it would be a serious loss were he through lack of financial assistance to give up or even to curtail the valuable work he has undertaken there."

George Pratt, an Amherst trustee and father of a boy who had attended Deerfield and Dickinson, made the lead gift of $35,000.

Fellow headmasters Lewis Perry, Al Stearns, and Horace Taft rallied to assist Boyden as well, a remarkable gesture since they were concurrently seeking badly needed gifts for their own institutions. "There is no doubt," Perry said, "that Deerfield is doing a unique and splendid work in American education I know of no school in

the country which I believe in more thoroughly than Deerfield Academy."

In December 1922 Perry introduced Boyden to Edward Harkness, the man whose millions pushed Exeter to the forefront of American secondary schools. "We did not ask him for any money directly," Perry said, "I told him that I just wanted Boyden to have a chance at telling his story. Two days later I received a splendid letter saying that he would give $30,000 to the school. I think what Harkness has done ought to encourage a lot of men who are interested in Amherst. If Amherst does not foster it, I am going to try to secure it for Williams." Within days of this initial pledge, Harkness decided to increase his contribution to $100,000 on the condition that it be matched by 1 April.

In addition to their Amherst ties, Boyden and Al Stearns both loved baseball. Captain of the 1894 squad that finished second in the national championship, Stearns was one of Amherst's greatest ballplayers. In later years the two headmasters enjoyed meeting at Fenway Park to "talk shop" and root for the Boston Braves.

In 1922 Stearns approached classmate Dwight Morrow of J. P. Morgan: "You may be a bit surprised to get a letter of this kind from me but I am very much worked up over first hand information which indicated that most estimable school is likely to smash on the rocks in the next few months if friends do not come to the rescue. My interest in the matter is very deep and sincere both because of the strategic position the school occupies with reference to Amherst College, and even more because of my confidence in its high character and standards, a feeling which I confess I do not share with regard to most of our modern educational institutions. Deerfield appears to be putting no shoddy in with its wool, and its product will stand the wear and tear of life in consequence." Morrow immediately wrote Boyden a check for $5,000.

Although preoccupied throughout the Deerfield and Dickinson buy-out with politics and money raising, Boyden maintained his daily commitment to quality schooling. In fact, the academy's educational stature seemed to increase as its political and monetary stakes heightened. This was no coincidence. From his earliest Deerfield

days, Boyden appreciated the correlation between his school's educational quality and its political leverage.

From Boyden's earliest Deerfield years, dances were essential both for teaching character and advancing the school's reputation as a vital community center. This emphasis worked as well in 1902 as it did twenty years later. In November 1922 when the academy's financial prospects seemed gloomiest, Joe Gibbs visited the Boydens. He found the headmaster conducting a school dance.

"This was a party for the boarding boys and the local girls," Gibbs wrote. "At the last party I attended at the Academy, all the girls were from Smith College. They were certainly a well selected and a charming group and the party was a delightful one. Last night as I saw the local girls coming in and laying off their wraps, disclosing their very simple little gowns, I wondered whether the boys would be as fine to them as they had been to the Smith girls a fortnight ago. I wish you could have been there. After all the girls came into the big living room in the new dormitory, Frank gave the signal and all the boarding boys, every one of them, came downstairs and as they did so the orchestra struck up for the first time. I expected a general and an awkward pause as the boys came pouring into the living room but to my delight and to my amazement the boys just dissolved to the sides of the room and actually within thirty seconds every girl had been taken for the dance. When this dance ended each of the boys stood by his partner with just the same deference that I had noted so delightfully at the Smith party a fortnight ago. It kept me awake for some time last night to think how the continued existence of this little pure democracy is threatened. It (the academy) is more than a local democracy, for these boys are going out to live their lives and to exert their influence in widely scattered communities throughout the country. Moreover, educators and others are making little pilgrimages to Deerfield and are going back to their communities carrying the germ with them. It just seems as though it could not be possible that the light should be permitted to go out in Deerfield."

Boyden was never bashful at school meetings about describing the school's fiscal or political needs. By sharing his ambitions and strategies directly with Deerfield students, he won their admiration and enlisted their support. No student could fault his headmaster for

trying to improve school food, buy athletic uniforms, and build a new gymnasium and dormitory. The winter issue of the school paper wasted little time taking Boyden's lead: "A special effort will be made to secure a large amount of money towards the gymnasium. The students will have the chance to make or mar this opportunity, and we all must do our very best to MAKE IT and make it WHAT IT SHOULD BE."

The spring *Pocumtuck* was more emphatic. "The very school itself lies in the hands of its students. We are in the midst of a $400,000 campaign for buildings. We must have this money if the school is to continue producing the type of boy and girl the world needs. It is the job of the students to 'Sell the School.' To do this every member must do his very best in his school work, on the athletic fields, and in his general business By completing the required work we can gain the money and the friends that the academy needs. This reward is too big to lose. We must take no chances."

Speaking at a town meeting in February 1923, the headmaster appealed directly to the Deerfield public. Ironically, the $100,000 Deerfield Academy and Dickinson High School trustees had borrowed to build new dormitories was Boyden's "ace in the hole." Although he was reviled by some townspeople for incurring this debt, most critics realized little money would be raised to repay the loan until Boyden reorganized the school on an independent basis. As the headmaster's legal counsel noted, "Its trump cards it seems to me are its heavy indebtedness . . . apparently the Dickinson trustees are forced to depend upon gifts which only Mr. Boyden or his friends may be able to secure." Were it not for this large debt, the town might have been inclined to take the school over.

Another significant consideration weighed heavily against the town's continued interest in Deerfield Academy and Dickinson High School. Regardless of its decision about the academy, a larger high school would be required within three years to accommodate the rapidly expanding population of South Deerfield. It would cost the town at least $200,000 to seize Deerfield and Dickinson, assume its debts, and also build a new school.

Boyden proposed an alternative solution. He planned to incorporate a new board of trustees of Deerfield Academy that would

purchase the school for $150,000 from the old Deerfield and Dickinson board. After settling the school's outstanding debt, the town would retain $50,000 as its share of the original Dickinson funds. This money could then be used to defray the cost of building a new school and maintaining the public library. With $50,000 in hand, Deerfield would face a more manageable expense of $75,000 for the new public high school.

While most townspeople agreed with Boyden, a few led by Harold Flower and Winthrop Arms dissented. Hoping to seize the school by eminent domain, they argued that the Deerfield and Dickinson trustees had exceeded their authority by borrowing money to open a boarding department. They contended that the individuals who endorsed those notes were personally liable and believed Deerfield's townspeople were not empowered to authorize the sale of Deerfield Academy and Dickinson High School. This power was reserved for the state legislature that approved the initial act of incorporation. Flower and Arms insisted the proposed Deerfield and Dickinson dissolution contradicted Esther Dickinson's charitable intentions. They also challenged the $50,000 purchase price because it was 30 percent less than Dickinson's original gift.

The proposed school buy-out prompted bitter debate. When the Flower faction circulated a pamphlet claiming Boyden was stealing the school from the town, the pro-Boyden contingent countered with this handbill:

"The pamphlet you have just received is an insult to your intelligence. It is an attempt to manipulate your honest opinion on a clear cut issue. Are you willing to have the will of the people clouded and even destroyed by legal quibbling? Have you analyzed the motives activating them? Can you point to any constructive piece of work for the village ever accomplished by them? Have you thought of the result to You of the Academy's destruction? Have you considered the result to Your property? How long will you stand for petty spite, trickery, quibbling, the manipulation of figures, and the autocracy of a few unscrupulous or uninformed citizens? DO YOU STAND FOR COMMON SENSE, HONESTY AND DEMOCRACY? Then think for yourself! Don't be fooled."

With the Flower litigation pending and the town divided, Boyden
scrambled to meet the April 1 deadline for matching Ed Harkness's
$100,000 pledge. In late March, when Tug Wilson, Boyden's prolific
money-raiser, fell seriously ill, the headmaster begged Al Stearns, "I
am willing to go anywhere at any time to see anybody if there is any
possible chance of their being introduced and my not being a
nuisance."

On 31 March, Stearns wired the Pratt brothers, Dwight Morrow,
and George Plimpton of Ginn Publishing, "Isn't it possible to get
together several Amherst men and others there in New York who can
and will put up in the form of a loan if necessary the amount
required to keep Boyden going and save for Amherst College and the
country what gives every prospect of becoming one of the soundest
and best preparatory schools? With all the sums of money that are
thrown into fake educational experiments, it would be a crime of
crimes to have Boyden go under at this stage."

When nothing came of this eleventh hour petition, Cleeland,
Maynard, and Frank Stearns agreed to underwrite the requisite
balance subject to Boyden's promise to secure their money in the
months ahead.

While the Deerfield and Dickinson buy-out enjoyed considerable
public support, its legal position was more doubtful. Boyden's plan
was suspect on several counts. Esther Dickinson's explicit intention
was to provide a "School of a high order free to all the children of
Deerfield located on my home lot on Deerfield Street." The
Deerfield and Dickinson trustees had clearly exceeded their authority
opening a boarding department. The Dickinson bequest also required
maintenance of a public library and reading room, a responsibility the
trustees had badly neglected since admitting boarders in 1916.

If these were not sufficient legal grounds to stop the buy-out, the
anti-Boyden faction further argued that responsibility for managing
the Dickinson bequest was assigned specifically to the school's
trustees. Deerfield's townspeople therefore had no right to dictate the
school's sale by popular vote, nor to apply money from this sale
toward construction of a new school.

Arguing for the defense, Boyden's counsel, William Davenport,
insisted admitting tuition-paying boarding students was the only way

Deerfield Academy and Dickinson High School could afford educating local children without charge. Based on its strong public approval, the Deerfield and Dickinson buy-out clearly was in the best interest of Deerfield's children. It consequently was in direct accord with the Dickinson bequest.

On 16 October 1923 the Massachusetts Superior Court authorized the buy-out. The Springfield *Union* reported, "In brief form the court found that a general charitable intent existed under the will of Esther Dickinson; that change of circumstances made it impracticable and impossible to administer the trust in the manner provided by the testatrix and that it was impossible to carry out the charitable purpose of the testatrix."

Hoping to prolong the litigation and undercut Boyden's fragile financial backing, J. Weston Allen tried to appeal. This maneuver nearly succeeded. Speaking for Cleeland and Frank Stearns, Maynard testified, "We three men had been working something like two years to raise this sum of $145,000 and had found it no sinecure. Some of the money had been conditioned on the reorganization going through by a certain date. As young men without large resources, we were not willing to assume the responsibility of furnishing so large a sum of money ourselves, which would be the case if we were unable to keep our contributors in line."

The Deerfield and Dickinson counsel objected to Allen's appeal, "stating that the existence of this litigation had been a source of embarrassment to the school and that his clients desired that the matter be disposed of immediately." The appeal was subsequently denied.

Although strict legal interpretation might have favored the anti-Boyden faction, the court's holding recognized overwhelming popular support for the academy. Reflecting later on his good fortune in this case, Boyden admitted manipulating the Dickinson bequest and the anti-aid legislation, albeit for the public good: "I had a talk with the Commissioner of Education with regard to the subterfuge which we worked and he seemed to think that it was perfectly all right."

While Boyden harbored minor reservations about the methods he employed, he had no doubt about the ends he had achieved. With

sufficient money and judicial approval to reorganize Deerfield Academy and Dickinson High School as a college preparatory academy, Boyden was a step closer to realizing his singular ambition. "My own feeling is that we are building up what may and we hope will turn out to be a big and famous academy," he wrote Bill Davenport. "Matters have been handled somewhat informally at times in the past, and these informalities have caused us some anxiety, to say the least, during the proceedings which we hope are ended. For the future I want to build firmly and permanently."

15

BEGINNING AGAIN

After twenty-two years leading a semipublic rural high school to regional prominence, Boyden's buy-out of Deerfield and Dickinson High School earned him the right to begin school-building all over again. In 1902 many hoped Boyden would fail. Now the stakes were raised and the earlier expectations reversed. A handful of personal friends had contributed $200,000 almost exclusively on their faith in the headmaster. This sum entitled Boyden to independent control of the academy, its property, and its obsolescent physical plant. It also made him wholly responsible for the school's success.

The first task for the newly incorporated academy was establishing a board of trustees. Maynard and Boyden consequently began searching for prospective members. They were fortunate in not having to look beyond nearby Adams, Massachusetts, the home of Charles T. Plunkett. Owner of Berkshire Cotton Manufacturing Company, a $2.5 million textile firm, Plunkett had just recently entrusted his nephew to Boyden's care. Although quite ill and convalescing in Florida, Plunkett agreed to lend his name and influence to the academy as its first president of the board of trustees.

Deerfield Academy's most pressing immediate need was a new dormitory. With public appropriations terminated and no endowment, the school relied exclusively on tuition and board to meet its operating expenses. To complicate fiscal matters, Boyden had agreed to continue educating local children at little or no charge as a condition of the buy-out. Faced with an immediate cash shortage, the headmaster boosted the academy's receipts by enrolling more students than he had dormitory beds.

In February Boyden wrote Plunkett, these "seventeen boys who were sleeping in the pool room on the top floor of the big dormitory

were getting restless." According to the Boyden code, the two best antidotes for restlessness were business and weariness. "Work 'em hard, play 'em hard, feed 'em up to the nines," he explained to John McPhee. "And send 'em to bed so tired that they are asleep before their heads are on the pillow." Without a gymnasium and sufficient dormitory space, this would be a difficult proposition.

Boyden temporarily solved the gymnasium problem by purchasing Segar Graham's old cowbarn adjoining the Ephraim Williams House for $750. He immediately put the boys to work installing a new basketball floor. "Mr. Boyden just loves to see us work," the *Pocumtuck* reported, "We scrape in unison."

In February, although the barn conversion was finished, Maynard suggested Boyden send Plunkett a picture of the students hard at work. "I will follow up your suggestion," Boyden replied, "and will endeavor to get pictures taken of the boys scraping even if the floor is already done." Hoping to persuade Plunkett to donate a new dormitory, Boyden sent him a staged photograph of the boys sanding the recently refinished barn floor. It took several months effort but Plunkett pledged the dormitory.

With money secured for the Plunkett Dormitory, Boyden continued to expand the boarding department, housing two dozen additional boys in the barn until the new building was completed. Boyden also launched a campaign to replace the decrepit Dickinson school building and construct a full-fledged gymnasium and swimming pool. In 1923 the headmaster had persuaded Bruce Barton to write some sales copy for the new academy as he had done for Amherst. The following year Barton made good on this agreement.

First published in the 1924 commencement *Pocumtuck*, Barton's "Deerfield and the New England Conscience" is one of the most cited texts in the academy's history. Barton, however, admitted knowing little if anything about Deerfield when he wrote it. This explains why his emphasis is long on New England and short on the academy. Rarely a procrastinator, Barton delayed writing the Deerfield text for an unusually long time before sitting down one Sunday afternoon to make "a start on the thing at last."

"There is something about Deerfield which is not easy to put into print," Barton wrote. "Something that you feel in the corridors of its

Frank Boyden as a child.

Boyden with Deerfield and Dickinson faculty members c. 1910.

*Frank Boyden
in his first years as headmaster.*

*No student better exemplified Boyden's vision for education than Tom Ashley
(seated in front row, second from left).*

*Jenny Arms Sheldon,
close Boyden friend,
academy benefactor, and
champion of education for girls.*

Boyden leading pregame infield practice.

Lewis Perry, headmaster of Exeter Academy; Boyden; and Claude Fuess, headmaster of Andover Academy.

Frank Boyden with President John F. Kennedy.

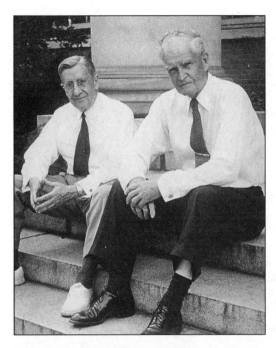

*Frank Boyden
and Bruce Barton,
legendary advertising
executive.*

Frank Boyden with President Richard M. Nixon.

Mr. and Mrs. Boyden, an unbeatable combination.

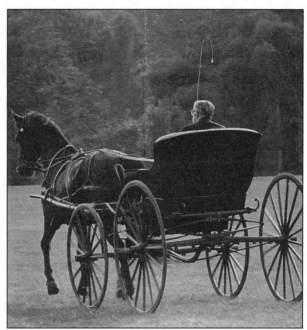

*Boyden
and his first love –
a horse and buggy.*

Boyden and students.

Frank Boyden
(Photo by Fabian Bachrach)

hundred-year-old buildings, and the atmosphere of its rugged hills. That something is the New England tradition, the presence of the New England conscience."

In later years the headmaster enjoyed joking about his Tennessee-born friend's interpretation. Boyden's own Yankee definition of New England conscience was "something that will not prevent a man from doing wrong, but will prevent him from enjoying it while he's doing it."

Still equivocating about the academy itself, Barton continued, "The men of New England birth or training have had an influence on our life far out of proportion to their numbers or wealth. They go to Washington, and somehow, power finds itself in their hands. They have spread across the continent, leaving colleges and white-steepled churches in their wake. They enter cities and rise to leadership. Somehow the granite of those hills has bred itself into their being. They stand firm and yield not. Men depend on them. The stuff which is in them does not crumble; institutions are established upon it.

"Deerfield is the cradle of that spirit," Barton concluded. "With money you may purchase buildings anywhere, and hire teachers, and say, 'Behold, this is a school.' But you cannot purchase or create the unseen something which is in those ancient halls. The souls of just men made perfect people its corridors; character covers the campus like a mantle; and the difference between what is right and what is wrong thrusts itself across the horizon as inescapably as Mount Tom. This is the stuff of the New England conscience, America's great asset and greater need."

Barton was initially dissatisfied with this work. "Here is a piece about Deerfield," he wrote Tug Wilson, "Is this what you want?" But Boyden loved it. Barton had described the essence of the headmaster's dream of a truly American academy in an authentic New England village.

While advertising guru Bruce Barton and textile magnate Charles Plunkett envisioned Deerfield Academy's future, Jenny Arms Sheldon maintained its links to the past. When the new board of trustees seriously considered turning the academy into an all-boy's boarding school in 1926, Sheldon alone preserved the interests of local girls.

Sheldon was a Vermont native by birth. Her mother died when she was five and Sheldon moved in with an aunt who lived in Deerfield. Sheldon attended the Prospect Hill School in Greenfield and was one of the first students at M.I.T.'s Woman's Laboratory. An active suffragette, she frequently contributed articles to the Boston *Woman's Journal*, the Springfield *Republican*, and the Boston *Transcript*. She later became a notable scientist, the first assistant to Professor Hyatt of M.I.T. After she married Deerfield's local historian, Sheldon became curator of the Pocumtuck Valley Memorial Association Museum.

Jenny Sheldon was elected a Deerfield and Dickinson trustee in 1913. She paid the rent each year for the academy's ballground out of her own pocket and advanced money on several occasions for new team uniforms. Interested as she was in Deerfield athletics, Sheldon was more concerned about Deerfield and Dickinson girls. In 1912 she offered to donate a new girls' club. But much as Boyden wanted the building, he balked at its restricted use. The headmaster suggested a billiard room be reserved in the club for boys' recreation. Sheldon held her ground. "I am deeply interested in the life of the Academy, social center work is another thing, and I do want the building to be a Girls Hall. I want it to stand for Work, Work, good thorough Work!" Ultimately constructed as Sheldon envisioned it, the girls' club was a handsome, badly needed addition to the school plant.

Through all the ups and downs of the anti-aid debate and the Deerfield and Dickinson buy-out, the Sheldon-Boyden association grew closer. Although she once berated the headmaster for failing to handwrite his personal letters, on another occasion Sheldon wrote, "It is needless to say you understand me and I understand you and we have absolute faith in each other." When Boyden needed to borrow $100,000 to renovate the John Williams House and build the school's first dormitory, Sheldon personally co-signed the note. Writing during the Flower litigation, Sheldon aptly predicted, "One thing is certain. If you live through this storm, you are good for fifty years."

After she died, Boyden described Sheldon somewhat unfairly as a simple, home-spun, kind-spirited lady. The headmaster enjoyed telling how Sheldon approached him in 1930 with her savings

account passbook. "I've been putting a little away," she said. "I'd like the Academy to build a science building and dedicate it to my father. I hope it's enough." Although this story tends to belittle her, Boyden meant no harm by it. Bruce Barton once told him, "It is very hard to get people interested in a school. You have got to create a legend that will appeal to the imagination." In Sheldon's case, Boyden believed the embellished story glorified both his friend and his academy. What better tale than that of a loyal country woman salting away her savings to build a badly needed building in her father's memory?

In truth, Sheldon planned to donate the science building in 1923, at the moment in the Deerfield and Dickinson buy-out when Boyden was in most dire need of funds. On 23 October Sheldon signed a will allocating money for "a building equipped for teaching chemistry, physics, geology, zoology, biology and botany and manual work." The following day she wrote Boyden, "When my father died in 1897 I knew what would be the most appropriate memorial to him, a scientific and industrial school. He believed strongly in this kind of an education. As the money was his, earned by hard work, I wish to have his memorial in harmony with his wishes. He was a mechanical man who believed in the kind of education that would make every boy and girl self-supporting."

Sheldon's will reflected her breadth of interests and great heart. She assigned money for education of blacks at the Hampton Institute and for women at Radcliffe College. She contributed to the Franklin County Hospital and the Free Religious Association of America. She left "income to be used for spraying and preserving the more than a century old elm on my homestead." She left $6,000 to Deerfield Academy for scholarships. Most significant, Sheldon left "$3,000 to Frank and Helen Boyden to be kept at interest until it is needed for the education of their children."

While Sheldon's science building was not an immediate trustee priority until 1930, fiscally responsible direction of the school's daily operation was. President of one of the largest textile firms in the northeast, Charles Plunkett expected Deerfield Academy to operate as cost-effectively as Berkshire Cotton. According to Bob Maynard, Plunkett believed "the school is a business venture" and "no business

venture can be run without businesslike methods of organization and control."

In 1925 some fifty local boys and girls were attending the academy entirely at the school's expense. Plunkett objected to admitting these children tuition-free. He insisted "we have no right to charge Tug Wilson full tuition for his boy Bill, and then to allocate a part of the money to paying the tuition of John Smith, who is worthy but indigent." Sheldon disagreed. Like Boyden, she believed "it is a good thing for the boys of the school to mix on friendly and equal terms with the boys and girls from the country, and an equally good thing for the boys and girls from the country to have the opportunity of rubbing elbows with the more or less sophisticated chaps who come to the boarding school."

Sheldon abhorred Plunkett's "dictatorial and big business-like way of handling the school." She realized charging tuition for local children would all but negate the possibility of their attending the academy. This was particularly true for girls, since parents were notably less inclined at that time to invest in educating their daughters. Expansion of Deerfield's all-boys boarding department further discriminated against local girls. "I will frankly say I am distressed about the girl situation," Sheldon wrote Boyden. "The Board of Trustees says it wants girls, and at the same time it brings about the conditions that make it well nigh impossible for girls to attend. As I told you two or three years ago, parents will not send their daughters to a school where boys are so much in excess. Every year we have more boys and less girls. I have tried to think this was a temporary undertaking, but it does not now appear to be."

Unlike Deerfield and Dickinson, Deerfield Academy concentrated more exclusively on educating boys. Although this bias was initiated by financial necessity, it subsequently reflected Boyden's increasing personal interest in teaching young men. The number of girls attending Deerfield consequently diminished until 1949, when the last girl of the Boyden era graduated. Were it not for Sheldon's insistence, it is likely girls would have disappeared from the academy by 1930.

Jenny Sheldon was the most loyal benefactor of Boyden's first twenty-five Deerfield years. But generous as she was, Sheldon could

not provide the financial leverage and social connections required to build the nationally acclaimed secondary school the headmaster dreamed of. Together with Plunkett, Boyden, Maynard, and Wilson began to replace Deerfield townspeople on the academy's governing board with more affluent American capitalists. As Boyden later told McPhee, "We needed more than poor Mrs. Sheldon and the onion growers."

Plunkett soon introduced Boyden to Horace Moses. One of Plunkett's industrialist colleagues, Moses was president of Strathmore Paper and founder of Junior Achievement, an extracurricular high school vocational-technical program committed to teaching American youth "The Blessings of Work and of Right Direction." When Plunkett died in 1927, Moses succeeded him as board chairman, a position he held for twenty years. For his part, Moses persuaded Ernst Behrend of Hammermill Paper and Howard Coonley of Walworth to join the Deerfield board.

While Plunkett worked his manufacturing connections, Boyden, Wilson, and Maynard plied the "old boy" Amherst network. Dwight Morrow of J. P. Morgan was their lead prospect. Supplying Amherst with blue-chip athletes was their primary hook.

"Deerfield is sending two pitchers to Amherst next year, and a number of football players, all of whom are A-1 scholars," Wilson wrote Morrow in 1926. "While the Commencement mood is on, would you care to speak to Mr. James and some of the others? I could name eight men who could give $25,000 this year but I do not wish to be always begging for Deerfield. You are one of the few that stand the pressure cheerfully." To encourage the academy's athletic program, several Amherst alumni donated perpetual trophies for outstanding play in football, baseball, and track. Of the fifty-one boys in Deerfield's Class of 1925, seventeen planned to attend Amherst.

Charlie Merrill of Merrill Lynch was among the Amherst men receptive to Deerfield's latest appeal. Although he eventually gave generously to the academy, Merrill began in 1926 with a modest $500 pledge, "to help some poor boy complete his preparation, training and then go to Amherst. I am awfully glad to do this because I had a pretty tough time squeezing through my last year of

preparatory school and I have a keen recollection of how worried and anxious an eighteen or nineteen year old boy can be." Boyden responded gratefully, "I never could have gone through college myself if it had not been for scholarship aid." Another intimate Boyden friendship and lucrative Deerfield association was forged.

A board comprised of successful businessmen has considerable advantages. As Boyden soon discovered, it also has its costs. Before long the board began to modify the academy's management style. This upset Boyden, who had run the academy by executive fiat for more than two decades. "For some reason or other for the last six months, I have seemed to be constantly getting in wrong with the committee," Boyden wrote Maynard in 1926.

Boyden was never unduly concerned with budgets and cash flow. Although generally aware of the school's financial condition because he signed all of its checks, the headmaster believed "Deerfield costs money." He preferred to buy now and pay later and somehow managed when pressed to come up with sufficient funds. Boyden chafed at the board's insistence on limiting his purchasing authority. "I have always ordered the books, laboratory supplies, apparatus, equipment, and every thing concerned with the internal management of the school," Boyden wrote. "It did not occur to me that any changes with regard to laboratory equipment or supplies or books came under the jurisdiction of the committee."

The headmaster fought to preserve his executive authority. "We have in six or seven years acquired the equipment and buildings which most schools spend from twenty-five to fifty years securing. Developments have been very rapid. Often quick action has been necessary because we are dealing with the health and safety of boys and not with materials." The board contended the academy's development required greater trustee involvement. Maynard insisted, "The school has grown to such an extent that it is physically impossible for you to do more than attend to the job of operating it and handling the boys. Someone else ought to be responsible for the details of ordinary business."

Despite persistent disagreement over management responsibilities, everyone concurred the academy must begin another fund drive as soon as possible. Preliminary plans called for a 1927 campaign in

recognition of Boyden's twenty-five years at Deerfield. Plunkett launched the drive with a $50,000 challenge gift. But the immediate response was disappointing. Many of Boyden's Amherst friends wondered if Deerfield would ever stop asking them for money. Just two years earlier they had put up a handsome sum to save the academy. Now the headmaster was back again begging. As willing as Morrow was to solicit gifts, he was reluctant to put up more than $10,000 himself. "Unresponsive as I seem to be to your many requests," he wrote Wilson, "I appreciate your continuing to ask me and I congratulate Deerfield on having a friend that keeps at it."

The board momentarily postponed the campaign and regrouped. It was clear Deerfield had to expand beyond its narrow Amherst support base if it hoped to meet its $1.25 million goal. Wilson consequently cast his net more widely. Although he failed to gain an introduction to Ned Harkness, Wilson persuaded his American Telephone & Telegraph colleague, vice president E. K. Hall, to head the drive. According to Maynard, "Tug thought Mr. Hall might do the trick and that he would certainly be an excellent chairman, having warm and widely extended friendships all over the country."

Hall and Wilson then assembled a campaign committee comprised of principals from America's most prominent businesses and universities, including AT&T; Kibbe Brothers; Lee, Higginson and Company; Batten, Barton, Durstine and Osborn; American International Corporation; Cheney Brothers Silk; J. P. Morgan; Walworth Manufacturing; Cross and Cross; Hills Brothers; J. C. Penney; R. H. Stearns; Root and McBride; Strathmore Paper; Southwestern Bell; Greenfield Tap and Die; Stoddard, Ball and Bartlett; Ginn and Company; Colgate; Cornell; Williams; Columbia; Dartmouth; Amherst; and Harvard.

The 1920s was a decade of unprecedented confidence in American business. This trend was amply reflected in the composition of Deerfield's new board and campaign committee. It was also apparent in the academy's shifting pedagogical emphasis. In 1928 a Deerfield *Scroll* editorial reported, "We have a democracy, a new nation, built by men with the same spirit for which we seek, built by manufacturers daring to try new modes of salesmanship, new methods of manufacture. It is the men with that spirit who are

making this country today, men prominent in education, politics, religion or any other walk of life . . . We ourselves need a spirit of progress, of pioneering, to make ourselves and our country what it should be."

Where Deerfield once envisioned itself as a flagship of rural education, it now began to cater to upper middle class city boys who aspired to lucrative business careers. Where the academy once took pride in its inclusiveness, it was gradually squinting toward elitism. "It is the inevitable rule of life that the strong and able shall lead those not so gifted," the *Pocumtuck* proclaimed. "It is the purpose of this school to turn out primarily only those who should in some way become leaders in our national life."

16

AMERICANIZATION

Frank Boyden envisioned Deerfield Academy as a crucible of American virtue, a school dedicated to nurturing the character and values essential for democratic citizenship. By 1915, however, children of European and East Asian immigrants were entering American public schools in unprecedented numbers. As Poles flooded the Pocumtuck Valley, Boyden feared his academy would be undermined by foreigners and first-generation Americans. Boyden refused to devote his life to running a public school for immigrants. He insisted he "could not afford to become Principal of a school which would virtually be a Polish high school."

Like Americans everywhere at this time, most Deerfield citizens viewed foreigners with great suspicion. If the Poles were not effectively assimilated into the American mainstream, Deerfielders feared they would establish a rival community capable of overwhelming their historic Yankee town. Deerfield consequently expected its schools to Americanize the immigrants. As one resident observed, "These men are here to stay. A public night school gives the best opportunity of acquainting these people not only with our language, but also with the meaning of our republican institutions and history. A denial of this privilege will merely postpone their introduction and may make it hostile instead of friendly."

Deerfield's initial "Polish problem" was compounded by the ensuing boom of first-generation-American babies. At a time when the town's native population was aging and its youth moving away, Deerfield's Polish families were growing. Before long, Polish children outnumbered native Deerfielders in the town schools. This represented both a dilemma and a blessing for Boyden's academy. Although the sudden influx of Poles threatened to dilute Boyden's

emphasis on an all-American education, it also amplified the importance of the headmaster's American focus.

Wilmot Trevoy, Boyden's Amherst classmate, described the headmaster's efforts to Americanize the Poles as a crusade: "In all these districts a battle is waging; it is about as well-defined as was the battle of the old pioneers in the early days of New England; then it was against deadly weapons, now against deadly ignorance; the struggle is in no sense against the foreigner himself, for it is evident that he has come to stay; what must be fought is the battle against his ignorance and the lowering of standards and tastes that would come if his ignorance were to triumph. Against such a triumph, Deerfield is standing as a successful bulwark. Under the leadership of the Academy, the old native stock is being sustained and strengthened and is standing its ground."

Although some Boyden critics malign the headmaster as a prejudiced xenophobe, the headmaster's sentiments toward foreigners merely echoed those of Americans nationwide. In the first two decades of the twentieth century, more than eight million immigrants ventured to the United States. Despite 1917 legislation requiring immigrant literacy, foreigners fleeing the First World War arrived in massive numbers. Confronted with over one million immigrants in 1920 and 1921, Congress enacted more restrictive immigration quotas. Immigration on this extraordinary scale made Americans uncomfortable. Deerfield natives were no exception.

Confronted with an explosion of Deerfield's Polish student population, Boyden planned to stabilize the declining enrollment of local natives by admitting "blue blooded" American boarding students. Since doubling the boarding department meant doubling dormitory space, Boyden began to raise money to build a new residence hall and to purchase homes on the town's main Street for conversion to dormitories. As Boyden told a colleague, "We put up dormitories that we might maintain the school as an American institution for the benefit of what American children there were in the town, and also as a means to help settle the Polish problem."

Boyden realized Deerfield lacked sufficient independent resources to finance these projects. He also recognized the importance of adopting a fund-raising strategy directed at an audience beyond the

academy's immediate constituency. Capitalizing on the xenophobic tenor of the day, Boyden presented his academy as a patriotic haven in an immigrant storm. "I truly feel as if Deerfield Street is one of the most wonderful places left in New England," Boyden wrote in 1923. "I think a society ought to be incorporated for its preservation which should also include the financing of Deerfield Academy in order that this institution may continue for many years to educate and train American youth so that they may remain on the ancestral homesteads and continue to keep the place of delight, pleasure, and education for thousands and thousands of tourists every summer."

Boyden excited local fears that the Polish who had initially settled in South Deerfield might soon purchase property on the Street. In the fall of 1923, Boyden and Bob Maynard purchased the historic Ephraim Williams House, which the academy subsequently used both as the headmaster's residence and as a dormitory. In November, Boyden invited William Sumner Appleton, director of the Society for the Preservation of New England Antiquities, to tour the house. Boyden hoped he might interest the well-connected antiquarian in Deerfield's historic preservation. Although Appleton commended Boyden on the purchase, he was unable to make the trip.

Boyden approached Appleton again the following spring. In the interim, the academy bought another old house adjoining school property. "We did not wish to purchase it," Boyden wrote, "but it was to be sold to a Greek to run as a fruit store, and since it had a real historic value, we feel it ought to be preserved." Boyden reiterated his concerns about immigrants owning property on the Street, "Somehow there should be found some way of securing money to buy these old houses as they are thrown upon the market, as otherwise Deerfield will go, as Hadley and Hatfield have, into the hands of the Polish and other foreigners." Boyden appealed to Appleton for help, "Each time as I stop and think of the number of people who have visited Deerfield and have gone into ecstasies over the old-time atmosphere, I feel there should be some way devised for getting money to preserve Deerfield for the whole country. Can you make some suggestions or do something along this line?"

Appleton remained uninterested. The antiquarian merely suggested posting a large sign directing visitors to the Memorial Hall Museum

located in the original academy building. Although money might consequently be raised from admission and voluntary contributions, it was insufficient to finance Boyden's ambitious dream. But lack of funds never stopped the headmaster from thinking big. To a great extent, it was the extraordinary scale of his ambitions and the unflagging conviction with which he pursued them that ultimately made the requisite money possible.

At the same time that Dr. William Goodwin approached John D. Rockefeller, Jr., with a plan to restore Williamsburg, Boyden embarked on a similarly bold enterprise at Deerfield. Shortly after Goodwin hooked Rockefeller, Boyden made a bid at interesting Henry Ford. "I really think the Henry Ford lead is worthwhile following up," he wrote Maynard, "unless he would want to run the whole town of Deerfield." Pausing for a moment to reflect on his own experience with local politics, the headmaster added, "Knowing Deerfield quite well, I should not worry much about that." When Ford opted to build his museum in Michigan, Boyden's plans for preserving Deerfield stalled until he was introduced to Helen and Henry Flynt a decade later.

Henry Flynt first met Frank Boyden in 1912, when his Monson Academy basketball team competed against Deerfield. Playing on its own floor, a hastily converted study hall, Deerfield drubbed Monson 35-15. One month later at Monson, Flynt's club returned the favor as captain Flynt scored twenty-two points in a 48-16 rout. Born in a central Massachusetts town not unlike Deerfield, Henry Flynt grew up in a family he later remembered as "gatherers." Although Flynt's father was in the granite business and ran a general store, his principal avocation was collecting clocks. Prompted by the memory of a childhood home choked with "buffalo robes, postage stamps, clocks, Oriental rugs, glass, ceramics and other things," Flynt vowed never to collect anything himself. But Flynt inevitably succumbed to his father's penchant for "gathering." He began collecting autographs of United States presidents and chief justices because they fit in his briefcase, unlike more bulky items like furniture or silver.

When Henry Flynt, Jr., entered Deerfield Academy in 1936, Boyden insisted on entertaining his parents whenever they were in town. In addition to their mutual interest in Henry's education, Flynt

and Boyden shared an interest the headmaster's horses. "You have made us feel so much at home," Flynt wrote Boyden. "I am afraid that we are becoming a nuisance by staying with you so constantly when we are in Deerfield. One thing I did while I was there that I didn't dare mention at the table was that I sneaked out and saw the horses."

In 1938 four Deerfield homes became available for purchase. This renewed Boyden's fear that the town might fall into the hands of "foreign" interests. "Please don't get alarmed and think I feel we should purchase all of these homes," Boyden wrote a trustee. "But it presents quite a question so far as the future of Deerfield is concerned, and I think we should do all we can to maintain it at its recent high level."

By 1939 Boyden had interested Flynt in Deerfield's historic preservation. "Another phase that should go along would be the acquisition in a quiet way of necessary land," Flynt wrote Boyden. "We discussed the proper agency for accomplishing this and felt that undoubtedly the school or the Historical Society would be the logical group." Flynt explored the possibility of purchasing the Deerfield Inn himself, but the price was too steep. The following year he joined the academy's board of trustees as its new chairman.

Flynt initially attempted to persuade John D. Rockefeller, Jr., and Henry Ford to finance Deerfield's historic preservation. When they declined, Flynt dug into his own pockets. On 31 December 1941, he wrote a $2500 check credited to Deerfield Academy's "Land Acquisition Account." The following year he purchased the Manning property as a gift to the academy. Flynt had taken the first important step toward realizing Boyden's dream of restoring Deerfield's celebrated past for posterity.

Although Boyden conceived Deerfield's boarding department and historic restoration in response to Polish immigration, it is unfair to describe the headmaster as an unusually prejudiced bigot. Unlike many Americans whose nativist sentiments were blatantly reactionary, Boyden's attitude was not so much anti-immigrant as it was ultra-patriotic. From the headmaster's perspective, Polish immigration only heightened his belief in education as an instrument for nurturing values essential for American citizenship.

"American standards must be maintained," Boyden insisted. "American institutions must be preserved. The freedom of the people politically, economically, intellectually, morally and spiritually must continue to be advanced. This is not a matter of a day or a year. It may be of generations. It may be of an era. It is for us here and now to keep in the right direction, to remain constant to the ideals. We need a faith that is broad enough to let the people make their own mistakes. Let them come unto knowledge and understanding by their experience. Little progress can be made by merely attempting to repress what is evil. Our great hope lies in developing what is good. One newspaper is better than many criminal laws. One schoolmaster is better than a legion of bailiffs. One clergyman is better than an army with banners. These are our guarantees of internal peace and progress."

17

ELITISM

Like all prep schools, Deerfield is sometimes criticized for its exclusivity. Among the critics of prep elitism, C. Wright Mills called private academies "the most important agency for transmitting the traditions of the upper classes." E. Digby Baltzell described how academies "differentiate the upper classes from the rest of the population." Peter Cookson and Caroline Persell explained how "prep schools operated as exclusive clubs," to which "Catholics, Blacks, and Jews need not apply." Although Deerfield is included on every list of elite American schools, Boyden's academy, unlike its "St. Grottlesex" rivals, was not conceived as an exclusive institution. Prejudiced as the headmaster was in his own peculiar ways, Boyden's Deerfield was arguably the most inclusive of America's elite private academies.

It is true that most American academies were founded or revived by an emerging patrician class eager to consolidate and advance its fortune. Although academies were educational institutions in principle, they functioned more like clubs in fact. The admissions process ensured a prominent, white, Protestant, upper-class, male clientele. The schools themselves provided an environment where affluent youth could prepare both individually and collectively for power.

The country day school Boyden inherited differed dramatically from this elitist model. In 1902 Deerfield Academy and Dickinson High School was more a public institution than a private academy. It had no affiliation with plutocrats and barely sustained the interest of the local farmers. It had difficulty recruiting students of any class. It was not a boarding school nor did it exclude girls. Boyden insisted against exclusion of any kind. He considered "the country high

school as the institution that can meet the interests of all the people of the town without denominational or other barriers."

Although Deerfield has been more recently identified as a premier boys' school, girls played a decisive role in the headmaster's initial efforts to salvage the academy. Although Boyden had difficulty expressing himself publicly to girls, he privately acknowledged their contributions. "Your class had a hard row to hoe in straightening out things after 1908 got through," he wrote Elizabeth Greene '09. "To this day the school feels the influence of the girls of your class. I guess this isn't very well worded, but I always meant to tell you sometime how I felt."

For over a decade Deerfield Academy and Dickinson High School girls outnumbered boys and women teachers outnumbered men. One of these early women instructors was "a Jewish girl" recommended by Harvard, where she "was unable to secure the type of position for which she was qualified because of her nationality." Indifferent to the denominational distinctions prevalent at other colleges and academies, Boyden hired her. "She was the best Latin teacher we have ever had." Boyden believed ability and character were the fundamental prerequisites for teaching or attending Deerfield.

Although Boyden's interest in Jews was unusual among headmasters, cynics contend this was part of his Machiavellian scheme for cultivating advantageous associations. This criticism is partially justified. For example, in the 1920s Boyden accepted a Jewish boy recommended by Charles Merrill, who graduated despite a dismal failing record. In this instance, the headmaster's ulterior motive was the academy's institutional relationship with Merrill, founding partner of Merrill Lynch, who was a generous Deerfield patron. On the other hand, admitting Jews had more risks than benefits, as the admissions standards of other exclusively WASP academies attest. To Boyden's credit, Deerfield accepted Jews well before any of its prep rivals.

Boyden's interest in socializing Polish immigrants is another significant departure from the "power elite" critique of American prep schools. While other academies excluded immigrants, Boyden welcomed them with few reservations. The headmaster's personal sentiments aside, external circumstances demanded a comparatively

diverse Deerfield community. Until the 1924 Deerfield and Dickinson buy-out, Boyden was legally required to accept all town children. But Deerfield's commitment to inclusiveness did not change dramatically when he acquired private control of the academy. Except for the few instances when the political or financial stakes were too great to overlook, Boyden considered individuals in their own right, independent of societal standards. For over fifty years a personal interview with the headmaster was the sole requirement for admission to Deerfield. Girl or boy, rich or poor, Protestant, Catholic or Jew, if you impressed Boyden favorably, you were accepted.

Girls gradually disappeared from Deerfield as the number of local school age children declined and the boys boarding population grew. In 1926 Boyden considered but decided against opening a girls boarding department. "I am very sure our trustees would not care to have a girls department in the school," he wrote Porter Sargent. "Our present arrangement is working out satisfactorily. I like having the girls as day students but do not at the present time care to undertake establishing a boarding department for them." This decision was not unusual since coeducational boarding schools were not generally accepted until the 1970s. But the girls who did attend Deerfield until the trustees officially excluded them in 1949 often blamed their second rate status. When asked for a contribution to the academy's annual fund, one alumna wrote, "I am not interested. It is no longer a school which admits girls and we were always inferior specimens there."

Deerfield girls' biggest gripe was Boyden's insistence on directing them into clerical, "pink collar" jobs rather than professional work. "I am very anxious for you to go into work eventually for which you are well qualified," the headmaster wrote a female member of the Class of 1920. "I wonder very much if you have got the physique and force necessary for a successful high school teacher, which is about all you would be prepared for upon graduating from Mount Holyoke. There are many fine openings now in secretarial work, or in library work which pay well and for which I think you would be particularly well adapted. The other course I have in mind for you in case you really want to teach is one in kindergarten work." Objectionable as this bias is by our contemporary standards, it was a sentiment shared

by most men of Boyden's day. By traditional prep standards, Deerfield girls were fortunate to receive an academy education at all.

Deerfield girls were doubly discriminated against both because of their gender and their nonresidential status. All Deerfield day students were held to a different standard than boarders. Day students were not invited to eat meals with residential students. They also were required to take an extra year of classes to compensate for the school time they missed living off-campus. Boyden had an unabashed preference for boarding students. When a day boy got involved in trouble, Boyden often attributed it to his nonresidential status. "He is not in our boarding department," Boyden wrote a trustee rationalizing one day boy's mischief. "If he had lived in the dormitories with the other boys, a good deal of nonsense would have been taken out of him."

Some Boyden critics contend Deerfield's day/boarding split was a mask for intraschool discrimination by social class. They argue the day department was comprised of local farm boys of lower social standing whom Boyden exploited to improve the academy's athletic prospects. The boarding department, on the other hand, was made up of well-heeled, Social Register types who would leave Deerfield ready and able to make their mark on the world. In fact, the social differences between day and boarding students contributed to school diversity. This diversity fostered a positive learning environment for most everyone. Unlike its St. Grottlesex counterparts, Boyden's Deerfield offered opportunities for more social mixing. Although the actual experience might have reinforced extant class distinctions, the results more often than not were a greater degree of mutual understanding and respect.

The merits of Boyden's emphasis on social mixing was most evident during the Depression, when the tension between haves and have-nots was greatest. One affluent alumnus remembers local farmers burning their crops in 1934 to comply with National Recovery Act guidelines:

"We could see the flames in the September dusk on the hills across the river when we came out of the Old Dormitory after the evening meeting. We didn't know what they were until a master told us. We

stood and watched and talked about the fires in the darkness. We didn't talk long because we didn't know what to say. Then as now, the sons of valley farmers were in school, in our classes, and on our football teams. They were bigger and more muscular than we were at fourteen, and slower spoken. They carried with them the strong, not unpleasant smell of the barn, as foreign to us city bred boarding students as a foreign language. They were good guys to play with. One of them broke my nose that fall, but I don't remember that it upset me very much, and I must say I don't think it did him either. When the farmers burned the crops in the barns, the fires seemed to us not wrong or mean or malingering but acts of wrenching desperation. The flames against the scarlet and gold hills spoke sadly to us of work and ashes, of people in a kind of trouble we didn't know anything about, and our friends' fathers who did what they had to do in the dark world across the river."

Boyden's insistence on accepting students regardless of social class posed a significant financial burden for a school that often struggled to make ends meet. "I am not quite sure that it is perfectly fair to charge up to parents who are able to pay full tuition an unlimited bill for scholarships," Bob Maynard wrote Boyden in 1933. "I realize that up to a certain point it is beneficial to the boys who pay in full to have the companionship and example of those youngsters which they would not have but from the scholarship aid. Nevertheless, almost everybody now has to make sacrifices financially in sending boys to private schools and there is I suppose a limit to how much of his bill should be for items only collaterally connected with board, lodging and teaching."

Despite the prohibitive cost of scholarship students, Boyden ignored his trustees' annual objections to unlimited financial aid. For over thirty years Boyden continued admitting students on a need-blind basis. He required parents simply to "pay what you can". Asking "what can you pay?" was not an issue until the mid-1950s.

The biggest source of discrimination at Deerfield had nothing to do with gender, ethnicity, class, or religious preference. It evolved from the headmaster's predilection for tall, virile, handsome boys who would embellish the academy's overall image and improve its

prospects for athletic success. When Porter Sargent recommended a talented but frail student to Boyden, the headmaster respectfully demurred. "I have looked over carefully what you wrote me about Todd. Practically all of our boys are big, strong, vigorous fellows. I think of the sixty-six boys, fifty-five must be at least five-feet, ten inches or taller. We have never had any boys with any physical infirmities, even slight ones."

Ad hoc racial discrimination was another problem that plagued Deerfield, as it did all prep schools. Despite the landmark 1954 Supreme Court decision in *Brown V. Topeka*, Boyden remained adamant that the first African-American he accepted be truly outstanding in his own right. The first of Deerfield's few African-American alumni did not graduate until 1959. But true to Boyden's high standards, this alumnus subsequently distinguished himself at Williams College and in an educational consulting career.

Like all headmasters, Frank Boyden expected Deerfield graduates to assume positions of civic leadership and power. But Boyden's expectations were broader than most critics of American prep schools suggest. As the headmaster's own career attests, character and ability are equally important prerequisites for power as birthright. Contrary to the power elite critique of prep schools as exclusive preserves of an entrenched upper class, Boyden considered education, both private and public, a vital mechanism for facilitating greater social mobility. Boyden consequently envisioned Deerfield Academy as a place where less advantaged individuals could share privileges typically consigned to the affluent class.

18

THE MIDAS TOUCH

Ambition is one requisite for success, ability is another. But neither ambition nor ability would have fulfilled Boyden's Deerfield dream without money, a lot of it. When Boyden first arrived in Deerfield he inherited a moribund institution with insignificant assets. When he retired sixty-six years later, he left an academy whose physical plant rivaled many distinguished colleges. Considered by some "the greatest educational pickpocket in the land," Frank Boyden had the Midas touch. *Newsweek* called him "a genius for persuading people to part with their money."

Long before Bruce Barton advised Boyden "to create a legend that will appeal to the imagination and differentiate Deerfield from other schools," the headmaster was hard at work cultivating the academy's public image. From the earliest Boyden days Deerfield was a well-organized, carefully packaged product. This was entirely by design. Boyden's strategy depended heavily on creating a favorable impression. "You always meet people a second time," Boyden told generations of Deerfield students. "Be yourself with everyone you meet, but be your best self, for you can be sure that before you have lived out your life you are going to meet again." Boyden knew raising money would be a lot easier if he crafted an "impressive" institution and then gave it maximum exposure.

Boyden's obsession with public appearances most likely originated at Amherst. As a poor boy among affluent classmates, Boyden was painfully aware of his lower social standing. But Boyden believed proper attention to essential social graces could bridge this discrepancy between the haves and the have-nots. Boyden was confident one need not be a Vanderbilt or a Rockefeller to act like

one. "Sometimes good form is an inborn quality and comes as second nature," he said. "Sometimes there must be diligent training."

Indoctrination for new Deerfield students began on the opening day of school. "All the boys were informed that Mr. Boyden would like to see them during recess," said Whitman Wells. "We all gathered in one of the small rooms of the old academy building and what was said has always made a great impression throughout all my life. We were told to form a single line and that Mr. Boyden wanted to show us how to greet a person, walk up facing him and really shake his hand as though you were glad to see him."

From a fundraising perspective, no Deerfield lesson was more important than Boyden's persistent emphasis on courtesy to strangers. Confident his boys would make a favorable impression, Boyden went out of his way to create opportunities for contact between visitors and Deerfield students. He deliberately refused to post signs identifying the academy because he knew their absence would force visitors to seek information directly from students. Boyden also rarely allowed Deerfield boys to leave campus. If parents wanted to see their child when school was in session, they had to come to Deerfield. This gave the headmaster yet another opportunity to sell his school.

Boyden was not content to wait expectantly for visitors and guests. He took Deerfield's athletic teams and glee club on the road in active pursuit of new markets. By scheduling contests with Andover, Exeter, Choate, Taft, and Loomis, Deerfield benefitted by associating with more established academies. By participating in the Interpreparatory Sings held each year at Carnegie Hall, Boyden introduced Deerfield directly to potentially generous "Big Apple" audiences.

These road trips heightened Boyden's compulsiveness about Deerfield's public image. Arriving at a rival school, the headmaster strategically positioned the tallest, most handsome boys among the first to disembark from the team bus. Likewise, at glee club concerts Boyden took great care in "the placing of boys and their lineup on the stage. It seems to me that is a vitally important thing both for the singing and the appearance of the Club." On one occasion the headmaster chastised Ralph Oatley for failing to attend to this important detail. "I spoke about this once or twice and yet we went

to Hatfield with such young and inexperienced boys on the end of the bass line and practically every strong boy was back in the third row!"

Boyden's frankness about Deerfield's monetary needs was shocking. In daily talks and in newspaper articles and editorials the headmaster told Deerfield students that their effort was essential to the school's fortunes. The *Pocumtuck* and the *Scroll* reflected Boyden's appreciation and control of the press for disseminating school propaganda. "Our *Scroll* is a publication in which I take the greatest interest," he wrote Lewis Perry, "because we let the little fellows feel important. I have told the editorial board that it must be a friendly, family newspaper about the daily life of the students, it is not intended to solve in a critical way the problems which have been with us from the beginning of time and which they do not have the background to discern."

Realizing Deerfield would not receive substantial donations unless he asked for them, Boyden was never bashful about discussing the monetary prerequisites for quality education. His favorite sales pitch was a variation on the traditional "you can't take it with you" theme. "Socrates," said Boyden, "once asked why it is that people spend all their lives amassing wealth but don't seem to find money for the education of their children to whom they will eventually leave it all."

Barton was even more blunt. "The dead take to their graves in their clutched little fingers only that which they have not given away," he wrote a prospective Deerfield donor. "What are you going to do with your dough? Wouldn't it give you a great kick to put up a building at Deerfield? A swell building, not very expensive. But it would last forever and carry your name down the ages. What good is more dough when you have enough?"

Boyden always solicited gifts from a position of strength. He knew benefactors rarely gave substantial money to institutions that conveyed an aura of weakness. As poor as the academy was at times, the headmaster never cut corners where the school's public image was concerned. "Deerfield costs money!" Boyden said time and again. Even when he was running the school on a shoestring, the headmaster insisted on fresh flowers in the academy building and dining hall and free meals for all visitors. "If we were to lower our

standards," Boyden wrote Bob Maynard, "it would take many years to build them back. Our strongest schools, including Andover and Exeter, have had terrific deficits."

Since good food was another crucial aspect of the Deerfield image, Boyden hired Frank Novak, a Vienna-born chef with cooking experience at the Ritz Carlton, the Biltmore, and the Copley Plaza Hotels. Novak soon became one of the most important men in Boyden's administrative cadre. The 1935 Washington's Day banquet was typical of Deerfield's emphasis on food. Despite the Depression, Novak prepared a lavish meal featuring "Grapefruit Betsy Ross, Cream of Mushroom Soup, Broiled Sirloin Steak Mt. Vernon, Salad Martha, Broiled Tomatoes, Chateau Potatoes, Independence Ice Cream, and Washington Pie."

Boyden's own rather shabby appearance was an ironic but calculated counterpoint to his compulsive insistence on Deerfield's impeccable image. Boyden's clothes would have been an embarrassment to any other headmaster. His suits were noticeably patched, his shoes worn out, and his topcoats moth-eaten and spotted with grease. To the uninitiated, little distinguished Boyden's appearance from a common beggar's. But when a faculty member suggested the headmaster retire his threadbare overcoat, Boyden just smiled. "That coat's raised millions for Deerfield!"

In an improbable but surprisingly effective way, Boyden's rumpled appearance heightened the interest of prospective donors. Although his unorthodox style contradicted basic fundraising precepts, Boyden would never be dismissed as a slick, glad-handing money-raiser. "People have always been willing to listen to me," Boyden said, "because I seem to be different from what many people think a headmaster should be." From a patron's perspective, Boyden was an earnest, penny-pinching Yankee schoolmaster who surely squeezed the most from every donation.

But clothes indeed do not make the man. Boyden's unlikely appearance was a mask for a wily money-raiser who knew far more than he let on. Where fundraising was concerned, no trick was beyond Boyden's conscience. When Lewis Perry first visited Deerfield, Boyden assigned students various specific tasks to ensure the best possible impression. Several handpicked Deerfield boys

were instructed to greet Perry, others to tour him about campus, still others were told to study or toss a football in appointed places along the predesignated tour route.

On another occasion, Boyden invited Charlie Merrill of Merrill Lynch to a buffet lunch, where the headmaster feigned institutional indigence and intentionally neglected ordering enough food. This was a notable departure from Boyden's typical emphasis on ample good food for all. "By the time we got through the line, the food was almost gone," Merrill said. "This is the queerest place. We bask in the tremendous warmth and hospitality of Frank Boyden, but we run out of food. He takes me to the Library, but there are no books there. Now we are invited for coffee at his house. Does it have any furniture?"

One of Boyden's closest friends, Merrill was among the few Deerfield patrons who successfully called the headmaster's bluff. In the early 1950s Boyden piled two Deerfield hockey players into his Cadillac and traveled to New York where he planned to ask Merrill to underwrite a new rink. Boyden invited the boys along to make a good impression and reinforce his petition. But he expressly instructed them not to disclose the specific purpose of the visit.

When Boyden arrived in New York with the boys in tow, Merrill knew his friend was up to something. According to the prearranged scheme, the headmaster excused himself to use the washroom before beginning the meeting. This left the boys momentarily alone with Merrill to make a favorable impression. But Merrill managed to persuade the boys to reveal the headmaster's intentions.

When Boyden returned, Merrill absolutely refused to entertain any conversation about hockey. This frustrated the headmaster to no end. After an unproductive forty-five-minute conversation, Boyden resigned himself to defeat, nodded to the boys, and turned for the door. As the party reached the threshold, Merrill put his arm around his dear friend's shoulder, grinned widely, and said, "By the way Frank. You'll get your rink."

Boyden's flair for storytelling was yet another reason people were so willing to listen to him. Lewis Perry recalls introducing Boyden to Ed Harkness, whose millions ensured Exeter's fortune. Perry remembers "Deerfield Academy was down-and-out" when he asked

Boyden to tell Harkness the Tom Ashley story. "I went home by the night train and when I got to Exeter in the morning Margaret said, 'Here is a nice letter from Ed Harkness.' All Ed said was, 'Thank you for letting me hear the story of Tom Ashley and here is a check for $30,000.'"

The headmaster frequently used stories to disarm prospective patrons. One of his favorites described a Sunday school teacher who was trying to instruct her pupils about the importance of sharing. One day she decided to ask each student to make an offering and speak an appropriate word. As an example the teacher made a sample contribution, then said, "It is better to give than receive."

Mary Jones led off the student procession. Dropping her pennies into the basket, Mary said in a clear voice, "The Lord loveth a cheerful giver."

Johnny Smith followed Mary. He gave his money and said, "Blessed are those that give to the poor."

After some delay, the next little boy approached the offering basket and dropped in his coins. His name was Bruce McPherson. Looking sadly after his departed pennies, Bruce said, "A fool and his money are soon parted."

Although Boyden's ambitions for Deerfield required sizeable gifts, the headmaster appreciated support of any kind. He certainly chased plutocrats but not to the exclusion of small donors. Bob Crow recalled Boyden driving a hundred miles out of his way to visit an alumnus whose annual contribution never exceeded twenty-five dollars. Nor was Boyden averse to rejecting large gifts from individuals who tried to buy his favor. Crow remembers an instance when Boyden refused admission to the son of a very wealthy man. When the headmaster said there was no room to house the boy, the father offered to rent a house. When the headmaster said he would have to hire a new schoolmaster, the father offered to pay the master's salary. But Boyden refused. "He didn't like the boy. Or for that matter the man."

Frank Boyden, like most successful salesmen, relied on personal savvy, a quality product, and brand loyalty. His charisma and conviction alone carried Deerfield through the difficult early years. As a Deerfield education evolved into a highly valued commodity,

Boyden skillfully positioned the academy in the market. As it matured, he was quick to capitalize on repeat business. Like any other activity, one is more likely to succeed at tasks one enjoys. Next to raising boys, Boyden relished raising money. The fact that he was soliciting funds for a worthy cause only heightened his interest in both.

19

SPORTS

Boyden's interest in athletics greatly exceeded his ability. But modest athlete that he was, the headmaster insisted on sports as the linchpin of academy life. Athletics kept generations of Deerfield students busy. They taught sportsmanship and fair play. They also represented a vital advertising medium for a school that always seemed to be raising money.

At Amherst, Boyden's friends laughed when he dared try out for the baseball team. But Boyden, even then, was little discouraged by failure. When he failed to make the baseball cut, Boyden threw himself wholeheartedly into Doc Hitchcock's intramural program. At Amherst, Boyden learned the advantages of "athletics for all," a philosophy he later perfected at Deerfield.

Always looking for opportunities to associate with sports, Boyden actively developed close friends who were athletes. Tug Wilson led Amherst track to the 1902 New England championship. Bob Cleeland captained the 1902 basketball club. Al Stearns of Andover and Charlie Merrill of Merrill Lynch were among the greatest players ever to wear Amherst baseball uniforms. There were few more fanatical Amherst athletic boosters than Frank Boyden.

Professionalism in collegiate sports was as troublesome in Boyden's day as it is at present. In the spring of Boyden's senior year, two outstanding Amherst sluggers were suspended from intercollegiate competition after playing semipro ball under assumed names. Amherst, Williams, and Wesleyan consequently enacted stricter eligibility requirements. They also agreed to rules dictating proper conduct for baseball coaches, players and fans. These rules embodied the precepts of sportsmanship and fair play that Boyden later insisted on at Deerfield. Spectators were restricted to the

grandstands and bleachers. Coaching from the bench or sidelines was prohibited, as were heckling opponents and cheering intended to rattle the opposition. Extreme courtesy toward visiting teams was expected on the field and off.

After graduating from Amherst, Boyden hustled back to Foxboro's sandlots, where he made the hometown team as a first baseman and number two hitter. A failure at college athletics, Boyden quickly made his local mark. In a series with Plainville, Boyden turned two unassisted double plays and scored five runs in a two game Foxboro sweep. In the season finale against Caton Brothers Shop, Boyden's lead-off hit sparked a six run eighth inning rally and a 15-14 Labor Day victory.

When Boyden arrived in Deerfield, his enthusiasm for sports was never keener. The headmaster quickly won his students' favor by tossing a baseball around. This was not a typical school principal. Boyden not only endorsed sports as a worthwhile enterprise, he joined in himself. For the first decade of his Deerfield tenure, Boyden justified playing on the baseball and football squads by citing the difficulty his small school had fielding an entire squad. But Boyden actually competed by choice. Nor was he bashful about playing the "glory" positions. Until Tom Ashley's arrival in 1907, Boyden batted clean-up and played quarterback. Considering the headmaster's modest talent, most opponents had little reason to protest.

Although Boyden preferred home runs, he was a singles hitter himself. Harold Grove remembers Boyden as "an excellent hit-and-run batter. He could call his shots, hit ahead of the runner and hit'm where they ain't. I recall his short line drives, just over the infield. Those thorn in the side Texas leaguers. And how he could bunt! You always felt that he must have had a cue instead of a bat as he dropped a bunt just out of reach of infielders." A small man incapable of hitting the long ball, Boyden considered bunting the great equalizer. "You can put your glove on the ball," he said. "There is no reason you can't put your bat on it. Any one can learn to bunt."

On the gridiron, young Frank Boyden insisted on calling signals. "In a game against Shelburne Falls," the 120-pound Boyden

remembers being "tackled, picked up, carried backward and dumped into my own end zone. A legal play at the time." Nearly seven decades later, the National Football Hall of Fame recognized him as the third recipient of its Distinguished American Award, a prize previously awarded Vince Lombardi. "For over sixty-five years he was a dominating force behind the secondary school's reputation for hard, clean play and true sportsmanship. His players were noted for all-out effort, gentlemanly conduct, and hospitable hosts. And their creed usually resulted in victory. He invoked the minds, guided the spirits, and uplifted the aspirations of several generations of young Americans."

Although Boyden's emphasis on sportsmanship originated at Amherst, it was further embellished by the 1905 national campaign to reform college football. In November a Union College athlete died in a game against New York University prompting the university's chancellor to lambast football as a "homicidal" sport that "exalted bulk over brains." After a similarly brutal contest between Columbia and Wesleyan, The *New York Times* advocated handing the offensive "ruffians" over "to the police for an assault with intent to do bodily harm." When Columbia decided to abolish football and Harvard threatened to do the same, President Theodore Roosevelt, a former Crimson gridder, called a White House conference to resolve the problem. In late December a special committee convened to revise football rules, "open up" the game, and eliminate unnecessary roughness.

E. K. Hall, a friend of Boyden's who later directed the 1929 Deerfield Building Campaign, was a New England delegate to this conference. Elected collegiate rules committee chairman in 1911, Hall helped introduce the forward pass and doubled the distance required for a first down. When he died in 1932, after twenty-seven years on the committee, the Deerfield *Scroll* praised Hall. "To every American who has followed the development of American sports, he was known as the man who was more responsible than any other for the present form of collegiate football. Originating the modern passing game and making football a game of speed and strategy instead of brute force, these were some of his accomplishments.

They have had a profound influence on the entire realm of college sport."

Boyden's personal association with Hall amplified his own emphasis on fair play. It also inspired him to experiment with the new rules. Deerfield teams were among the first in secondary schools to capitalize on the forward pass. This early preference for "razzle dazzle" play helped early academy teams compensate for deficiencies in size and numbers. Deerfield clubs also invariably reflected the premium their headmaster put on sportsmanship. This is best expressed by a citation Boyden received in 1953 from the Sportsmanship Brotherhood: "Keep the Rules. Keep Faith With Your Comrade. Keep Your Temper. Keep A Stout Heart In Defeat. Keep Your Pride Under In Victory. Keep A Sound Soul, A Clean Mind, and A Healthy Body. Play The Game."

One of the best examples of Boyden's commitment to sportsmanship was an agreement with Horton Batchelder of Loomis that all Deerfield-Loomis contests be officiated by teachers. In 1930 Batchelder wrote Boyden, "I think you know my strong feeling that we shall never reach the ideal of sportsmanship until we play our games with amateur officials and leave the direction of play to the boys themselves. The only quarrels we ever have with officials are with paid men." The two headmasters subsequently agreed to "trust our boys to run their own games. By all means, if there seems to be a mistaken decision, let us stop the game and talk about it."

As early as 1908 the *Boston Globe* reported Boyden's unusual predilection for correcting officiating decisions that unfairly benefitted Deerfield. In one memorable contest, the 1945 baseball team put its undefeated season on the line in its final game against Wilbraham. Before the contest, despite unseasonably cold temperatures, the sixty-five-year-old Boyden removed his blazer and knocked out infield practice as was his pre-game custom. After nine innings the score remained tied. In the top of the eleventh, with a Deerfield runner on third, the rattled Wilbraham pitcher clearly hesitated in the middle of his motion. When the umpire correctly called a balk and waved the winning run home, Deerfield fans celebrated. But Boyden preferred to win by more "sporting" means. He rushed onto the field hoping to decline the balk and return the

Deerfield runner to third. Despite Boyden's animated protest the umpire upheld the call and Deerfield preserved one of the most memorable unbeaten seasons in its history.

Although Boyden personally preferred baseball, the headmaster considered basketball the sport in which the entire school, players and fans alike, could best participate. On Saturday evenings throughout the winter, all Deerfield students and faculty were required to assemble, sing the national anthem, and root for the home team. Many Deerfield victories were in fact attributed to school support. According to the 1921 *Pocumtuck*, "The most satisfactory sport for the school as a whole is basketball as it offers such a fine opportunity for the display of true sportsmanship on the part of both the team and the school. This year we have had one of the best teams in our athletic history and never has the singing and cheering been so good. Our orchestra was a great help at the games and no one will ever forget the singing when everyone was doing his best to cheer the team to victory. Often at critical moments the players won out largely through the earnest support given by the cheering section."

Although Deerfield's present fieldhouse rivals those of many colleges, this was not always the case. For Boyden's first twenty-two years, Deerfield played its basketball games on the top floor of the old Dickinson High School building. Harold Grove remembers: "Up in the attic was that long, very, very narrow gym floor. Right in the middle of the hall on the south side was a stage. The rounded front of this stage arched well out into the playing surface. The stage cut down the already narrow width of the floor quite materially. We used to call it the hour glass floor. There were big beams across the ceiling not much over ten feet above the playing surface. Roy Winn had a beautiful high arch in his long shots and shot over the beams. Ed Walsh used to bank his shots no matter where he shot from. The ball going at a terrific rate would hit the old chicken wire backboards, bounce back and forth, shiver about five or six times and then drop neatly through the hoop."

In 1924 Deerfield hoops moved to a converted horse barn the *Scroll* described as "palatial." But "when bleachers were put up all across the south side, the playing space became quite limited. The scorer often watched the game seated on one of the cross beams.

The smaller members of the student body and town children lay prone on their stomachs under the bleachers, peeping through upper classmates legs with their head cradled in their arms."

A master at cultivating Deerfield's public image, Boyden considered athletics his most dramatic showcase. At a time when the school could ill afford it, Boyden outfitted Deerfield teams in the finest uniforms available. Before long, local public schools began inquiring about the academy's discarded garments. "The rumor that we have new uniforms every year is without foundation," Boyden wrote the principal of Orange High School. "We do buy some uniforms each year for the first team but they are passed on the following year to the lower teams. At the present time we have nothing available as we helped the Deerfield High School at South Deerfield; possibly we may have some old shoes."

Uniforms alone did not ensure either a favorable impression or a winning season. Boyden consequently recruited athletes aggressively. His preference for tall strapping boys who could carry Deerfield teams to victory was legendary. In 1921, his loyalty to Amherst aside, Boyden refused to admit President Meicklejohn's sons because they were "too young for any work which we do and also too small in size." This shocked Horace Taft, who had incorrectly "supposed that your boys were about the same size as ours."

Because older boys enjoyed a considerable strength advantage, Boyden teams always had their share of repeat seniors and postgraduates, most of whom were local farm boys. Tom Ashley is a good example. On one occasion Boyden stopped Bernie Redmond as he boarded the bus for an afternoon away game. Bernie was a Deerfield native who had been doing farm chores since four that morning. Eleven hours later, as the team planned to depart, Bernie's beard sported a day's stubble. Concerned as always about his player's appearance, Boyden asked Bernie why he hadn't shaved that day. "I did," Bernie insisted. Noticeably upset, the headmaster replied, "Bernie, you look like you're twenty-one." "Mr. Boyden," Bernie said with a smile, "I AM TWENTY-ONE!"

Boyden believed in sports as a primary means of building character. "You can see the obvious things that football, cross country and soccer teach, such as physical courage or teamwork, but

there are a couple of things that might slip by. One thing is a sense of loyalty. A sense of loyalty makes a group a winner, and there's no better way to develop it than in athletics. Another thing is self-discipline. You've heard a lot about desire in players, the will to win. That desire has to become developed through self-discipline. Sacrificing time to practice, sacrificing a few bumps and bruises. You can't find discipline in better form than on the playing field. The best thing for boys is to strive to be the best, to want to win and be a success. You can't win all the time, and boys have to learn that too, but they should never stop trying to get up after they've been knocked down."

Boyden also endorsed athletics as a constructive way to occupy students who might otherwise get themselves into trouble. As Boyden himself once told a *Sports Illustrated* editor, "There is no doubt that one of the greatest helps in solving our problems of delinquency is more participation in athletics. I have had the privilege for more than fifty years to coach athletic teams in three sports and feel the real solution to most of our problems lies in the proper physical outlet and control of our teenage boys and girls."

Building on Hitchcock's Amherst model, Deerfield required athletics for all students regardless of ability. To this day, the academy offers eight soccer teams in its continuing Boyden-inspired commitment to appropriate competition for everyone. But despite its schoolwide emphasis on athletics for all, Boyden's Deerfield maintained a disproportionate interest in its varsity squads.

On alternate seasons, when the football team traveled to Connecticut to play Choate, the entire school went along to cheer them on. Arriving by train in downtown Wallingford, the student body marched in pairs to the playing field. According to the *Scroll's* report of the first all-school Choate trip, "Few will not remember marching down to the Choate field in a body with the band blaring forth ahead, feeling as organized, unified and as important as if it were a parade up Fifth Avenue. This particular part of the day was a success and showed clearly the value of organization." Lest there be any doubt, it was headmaster Boyden who controlled that organization, right down to the most minute details. "Topcoats over right arms with lapels facing outward, snappy rhythm, perfectly

coordinated ranks, spirited cheering, pageantry, this is the result of a deliberately planned campaign, an exhibition of military genius."

Try as he might, Boyden could not always control everything. One of the headmaster's favorite football stories described a moment when his best made plans were foiled. "We were behind in a game by three points late in the fourth quarter. We were driving and had the ball on the opponents' thirty yard line, first and ten. Then I looked out on the field and our quarterback was being carried off on a stretcher. I had no choice. I had to play Buckley, a boy who'd had little experience all year.

"As soon as the first play was under way, I could see that the young boy had called play number thirteen, even though I had thrown this play out after the first game because it was never successful. I had told our quarterbacks many times, never use number thirteen again. And now, in the big game, in a tight spot, here was Buckley, a greenhorn, calling the worst play in the book, number thirteen. I could do nothing but turn my back and cover my eyes. Then I was surprised at the great roar that went up from our fans. I looked up just in time to see Buckley cross the goal line with the winning touchdown. Bedlam broke loose and the team carried me off on their shoulders.

"Afterwards, when the locker room had quieted down, I went over to Buckley and said, 'Son, nice game. But tell me, why did you ever call number thirteen?'"

"'Well, coach,' Buckley replied. 'I saw Lewis coming out. His number was six. And my number was eight. So I guess I just totaled 'em up and used the answer. I called play thirteen.'"

"'Buckley,' I said with a hint of irritation, 'don't you know that six and eight are fourteen?'"

"Buckley just smiled sheepishly and said, 'Gee Mr. Boyden, if I was as smart as you, we would'a lost the game!'"

20

SINGING

Sportsman that he was, Boyden believed singing was almost as important as athletics. Whether at weekly Sunday meetings, in the bleachers at athletic contests, or at glee club concerts, Deerfield singing was a matter of great importance. Like athletics, Boyden considered singing a primary means for solidifying school spirit and for advertising the academy to a wider audience.

As an Amherst alumnus, Boyden was no stranger to the power of song. His alma mater boasted one of America's first collegiate glee clubs. His classmate, Jason Pierce, wrote the Amherst fight song. According to Claude Fuess, "on Tuesday evenings Amherst fraternities would emerge on to their respective verandahs and burst into song." Wherever three or four Amherst men come together, Fuess said, "they are likely to join the old favorites, 'I've been Working On The Railroad,' 'Who Killed Cock Robin,' or 'Lindy, Lindy, Sweet As Sugar Cane.'"

Singing was an Amherst tradition Boyden consciously transplanted at Deerfield. Within a year of Boyden's appointment as headmaster, academy students "realized the value of school songs and cheers in keeping up a good, lively school spirit." One of Mary Eddy's most pleasant memories of the Class of 1906 was "sitting on the academy building stairs singing 'Juanita' and other songs of that happy era." Edwin Preble '08 likewise enjoyed "looking back to those days of the old building, a rainy noon time, and the students gathered on the steps leading to Dickinson Hall, singing college favorites and "hits of the period, and as always Mr. Boyden mingling with the crowd."

Boyden considered singing the single best index of school morale. Singing also was an activity that bound all Deerfield students and alumni together. According to the *Scroll*, "One of the aspects of

boarding school life which has perhaps the most significance in reflecting the spirit of the school is the Sunday evening hymn singing. At 8:00 the boys and the faculty gather in the living room and sing the old hymns which help cultivate the spirit of things that are worthwhile and lasting. Wherever the boys may be away from school in years to come, they will remember on Sunday evenings that in the school living room the boys and teachers are singing the hymns which have become a part of all of us."

Boyden established the Deerfield glee club both for pedagogical and financial reasons. As the academy's enrollment grew, the headmaster was confronted with a shortage of athletic facilities and a growing number of boys who were not athletically inclined. Boyden utilized the glee club to relieve pressure on the school's overextended physical plant while concurrently providing a worthwhile activity for less athletic students. Not coincidentally, Deerfield's glee club, like its sports teams, became ambassadors to the general public and to prospective benefactors.

In 1923, when Boyden was struggling to raise money for the Deerfield and Dickinson buy-out, he asked fraternity brother Ralph Oatley to organize the club. This was a controversial appointment because Oatley had dropped out of Amherst in 1921 at least in part due to bad debts and a persistent alcohol problem. Trying to convince Boyden of his error, another fraternity brother referred to Oatley as a "swell headed little bluffer." But Boyden had confidence in Oatley's ability to coordinate a first-rate glee club.

The headmaster's judgment in this case was typically correct. Under Oatley's direction the glee club won five out of the first eight interscholastic glee club contests held each spring at Carnegie Hall. This success prompted Boyden to commend Oatley, "I have had the very deepest interest in the Glee Club since it started and each year have arranged for an increasing amount of money and time for its development. I have felt it was one of the soundest and best investments which the school has made. It has meant a great deal in the lives of hundreds of boys and also has helped to establish the right kind of contacts with other schools. I realize this has been largely due to your outstanding work and ability."

According to the *Scroll*, Deerfield's first glee club "made up in spirit what it lacked in ability." The club consisted of about twenty-five members, all of whom towered above their director. "They looked like a football team," Oatley said. "And they sang like one." At the club's first public appearance in 1924, "one enthusiastic member was so carried away by the applause of the audience after the first number that he himself vigorously burst into applause."

Oatley recalled other concerts at Charlemont, Amherst, Northfield, and the Franklin County Jail: "The interludes in the programs in those days were not, shall I say, similar to those of today. Instead of a bit of Chopin played by piano virtuoso, our first 'break' was filled in by Phil Mayher and Charlie Wellman singing 'Romeo and Juliet.' The audience would go into paroxysms of laughter over the 6-foot, 6-inch Phil as Juliet and 5-foot, 1-inch Charlie as Romeo. Between the second and third groups, Stu Pike bedecked in a pink sunbonnet would sing, 'No, John, No!'"

Ralph Oatley was a taskmaster. "Project you turkeys, project!" he implored his club. "Your voices don't even get over the footlights. Put some guts in it! OK, go back and try it again. You'll do it over until you get it right. Even if it's midnight." But Oatley was a perfectionist largely because Boyden demanded it. On one occasion, the headmaster berated him for what he considered a subpar effort, "It was a good performance and we undoubtedly were better than the other clubs, but it was not anywhere nearly up to our standard!"

On another occasion, Boyden threatened to cancel a concert before allowing anything short of excellence. "I should be absolutely unwilling to have the club go to Exeter," he wrote Oatley, "or any of the other schools with which we have striven so hard to make connections, and have them give a mediocre concert. Dr. Perry has talked so much about our boys that I should be unwilling to have them go there unless they gave a concert which was really outstanding."

As concerned with the club's appearance as he was with its singing, Boyden dictated each boy's position on stage for maximum effect. When a trustee commended him on the club's third consecutive victory at the Interpreparatory Sing, Boyden replied: "We had a fine time in New York and won first place again. Of

course we were pleased to rank first but we were even more delighted with the appearance of the Club and the manner in which they conducted themselves. There was not the slightest confusion or difficulty. A good many alumni came and we had a pleasant reunion."

Thanks in large measure to Ralph Oatley, Deerfield's glee club became one of Boyden's most effective tools for introducing the academy to prospective donors. After winning the 1930 New York Sing, Bob Maynard wrote the headmaster, "I received a telegram from you Sunday forenoon reading: 'We now, Margin fourteen.' At first I was inclined to hope that the margin referred to had to do with the capital campaign, but it later occurred to me that the Glee Club was probably in action Saturday night and had given a good account of itself again. I guess the operator turned the word 'won' over on its back. At any rate, I was more than pleased to know that Deerfield had carried off the honors once more and I am hopeful this success may have influence on the campaign."

In addition to its public relations function, the glee club was a celebrated source of Deerfield spirit. When it returned to "town late that Sunday night" after winning its first New York Sing, "the school and town folk lined the streets and cheered as their heroes came off the train and marched through town to the school." To this day, "The Even Song" and "The Sons of Deerfield," which Oatley composed in the 1920s continue to unify students, alumni/ae, and friends of Deerfield.

21

FACULTY

No headmaster asked more of his faculty than Frank Boyden. A benevolent despot who put the academy's interests ahead of everything else in his own life, Boyden expected the same from faculty. Although he asked no more of them than he asked of himself, Boyden's obsession with Deerfield set a standard that bordered on unreasonable. "I'm not running the school for the faculty," Boyden said. "I'm running it for the boys."

The first quality Boyden demanded from faculty was character. This was consistent with the premium Deerfield placed on molding men before minds. As far as formal knowledge and basic academic skills were concerned, the headmaster believed, "A person needs to pick up enough of the things that are needed in life. What those things are, I don't know."

Boyden was more concerned with values than lesson plans. "The success this school has had," Boyden said, "has been due to thorough grounding not only in basic academics but, almost more important, in training boys' attitudes toward life which will persist long after the precise details of booktraining have dimmed."

Boyden shared Gifford Pinchot's opinion on this subject: "Half a century of experience in executive work has proved to me that the first condition of success in any job is not brains but character. Over and over I have seen men of moderate intelligence come to the front because they had courage, integrity, self-respect, steadiness, perseverance and confidence in themselves, their cause and their work."

Among the many aspects of faculty character, Boyden valued loyalty before all else. "If you work for a man," Boyden said, quoting Pinchot, "in heaven's name work for him; stand by the

institution he represents. Remember, an ounce of loyalty is worth a pound of cleverness. If you must growl, condemn, and eternally find fault, resign your position. But as long as you are part of an institution, do not condemn it. If you do, the first high wind that comes along will blow you away."

On one occasion Bob McGlynn, an esteemed Deerfield English teacher, considered teaching at a rival prep school that promised to double his salary. Although he decided to stay at Deerfield, Boyden rewarded McGlynn's prospective disloyalty by refusing to raise his salary the following year. This was the only time in McGlynn's thirty-year career that he did not receive a raise.

From the day he arrived in Deerfield, Boyden envisioned the academy as an extended family. Practically speaking, achieving this ideal required faculty to accept round-the-clock responsibilities. As a surrogate parent, the Deerfield schoolmaster's job never ended. The academy's daily schedule made sure of this.

7:30	Breakfast
8:15	Outside Bell Rings
8:15-8:27	Classes Pass
8:30-9:12	First Period
9:15-9:57	Second Period
10:00-10:42	Third Period
10:45-11:27	Fourth Period
11:30-12:12	Fifth Period
12:30	Lunch
1:00	Meeting in Boyden's Living Room
1:30-1:32	Homeroom
1:32-1:35	Classes Pass
1:35-2:17	Sixth Period
2:20-3:02	Seventh Period
3:05	Athletics
5:45	Dormitory Room Inspection
6:00	Dinner
7:10	School Meeting

FACULTY

No headmaster asked more of his faculty than Frank Boyden. A benevolent despot who put the academy's interests ahead of everything else in his own life, Boyden expected the same from faculty. Although he asked no more of them than he asked of himself, Boyden's obsession with Deerfield set a standard that bordered on unreasonable. "I'm not running the school for the faculty," Boyden said. "I'm running it for the boys."

The first quality Boyden demanded from faculty was character. This was consistent with the premium Deerfield placed on molding men before minds. As far as formal knowledge and basic academic skills were concerned, the headmaster believed, "A person needs to pick up enough of the things that are needed in life. What those things are, I don't know."

Boyden was more concerned with values than lesson plans. "The success this school has had," Boyden said, "has been due to thorough grounding not only in basic academics but, almost more important, in training boys' attitudes toward life which will persist long after the precise details of booktraining have dimmed."

Boyden shared Gifford Pinchot's opinion on this subject: "Half a century of experience in executive work has proved to me that the first condition of success in any job is not brains but character. Over and over I have seen men of moderate intelligence come to the front because they had courage, integrity, self-respect, steadiness, perseverance and confidence in themselves, their cause and their work."

Among the many aspects of faculty character, Boyden valued loyalty before all else. "If you work for a man," Boyden said, quoting Pinchot, "in heaven's name work for him; stand by the

institution he represents. Remember, an ounce of loyalty is worth a
pound of cleverness. If you must growl, condemn, and eternally find
fault, resign your position. But as long as you are part of an
institution, do not condemn it. If you do, the first high wind that
comes along will blow you away."

On one occasion Bob McGlynn, an esteemed Deerfield English
teacher, considered teaching at a rival prep school that promised to
double his salary. Although he decided to stay at Deerfield, Boyden
rewarded McGlynn's prospective disloyalty by refusing to raise his
salary the following year. This was the only time in McGlynn's
thirty-year career that he did not receive a raise.

From the day he arrived in Deerfield, Boyden envisioned the
academy as an extended family. Practically speaking, achieving this
ideal required faculty to accept round-the-clock responsibilities. As
a surrogate parent, the Deerfield schoolmaster's job never ended.
The academy's daily schedule made sure of this.

7:30	Breakfast
8:15	Outside Bell Rings
8:15-8:27	Classes Pass
8:30-9:12	First Period
9:15-9:57	Second Period
10:00-10:42	Third Period
10:45-11:27	Fourth Period
11:30-12:12	Fifth Period
12:30	Lunch
1:00	Meeting in Boyden's Living Room
1:30-1:32	Homeroom
1:32-1:35	Classes Pass
1:35-2:17	Sixth Period
2:20-3:02	Seventh Period
3:05	Athletics
5:45	Dormitory Room Inspection
6:00	Dinner
7:10	School Meeting

Boyden believed the more students and faculty associated the better. "What we need more than ever," he insisted, "is persistent contact of boys with teachers; teachers who are sympathetic, firm, encouraging and soundly imaginative."

While other prep schools like Andover and Exeter emphasized schoolwork, Deerfield accentuated residential life. All Deerfield meals, including breakfast, were served by a faculty member "family style." All dormitory corridors were supervised each evening by their respective resident schoolmasters. Where other headmasters put a premium on quality teaching, Boyden exhorted Deerfield faculty to "consider dormitory work a real job. Study it as you would a business. Have an occasional corridor meeting. Build up corridor spirit and know each boy intimately. Hold each one to the highest standard he can maintain."

Although knowledge and teaching ability were expected of any schoolmaster, Boyden believed, "A fellow with just brains often becomes a little too self-centered and cynical." Sense of humor, sympathy for the problems of youth, personality, a mind receptive to new ideas, an optimistic philosophy of life, and a hobby were the qualities Boyden valued most in his faculty.

The frenetic pace of Deerfield life took an enormous toll on faculty. Several outstanding teachers left for institutions more sympathetic to their cerebral dispositions, as did many married couples who were unwilling to subordinate their personal lives to Boyden's rigorous expectations. In fact, until World War II interrupted the supply of bachelor schoolmasters, Boyden considered marriage probable grounds for dismissing a Deerfield faculty member.

To Boyden's credit, for every schoolmaster who balked at Deerfield's interminable duties, there were more who embraced them wholeheartedly. Loyalty cut both ways. As much as Boyden expected of his faculty, he also backed them to the hilt. "He has no patience with minor failings," said one forty-year Deerfield teacher, "But with big failings he has infinite patience." Boyden himself insisted "people who want to feel behind them the security and power of this school should be made to realize they must commit

themselves to the purpose of this school regardless of the inroads this may make on their own social program!"

Boyden had a flair for convincing faculty that no job was more important than teaching. He also knew when it was most effective to delegate authority. As much as the headmaster imposed on faculty members' personal lives, he steered clear of their classrooms. For better or worse, Deerfield teachers were free to teach as they pleased. "I'm better at running the baseball team and the office," Boyden said.

Having decentralized teaching itself, Boyden retained responsibility for hand-delivering grades to each student and reporting academic progress to parents. In so doing, he added yet another instrument for motivating students while concurrently monitoring, if not controlling, teachers. A Deerfield teacher was unlikely to grade harshly knowing the headmaster had to deliver the bad news. Deerfield teachers also realized the headmaster used these grade-giving sessions to survey student opinion about the faculty.

Deerfield, like all prep schools, expects its faculty to subordinate themselves to the collective interests of the school. In exchange, it offers a simplified but demanding term-time lifestyle offset by generous vacations. Because there is rarely a shortage of individuals eager to teach in prep schools, even the very best prep schoolmasters are considered replaceable. This is particularly true among the most prestigious institutions. Frank Boyden understood these market dynamics and consequently pushed his faculty to the limit and beyond. Although he lost several superior instructors, the headmaster convinced many more to do his bidding. The fact that so few faculty left despite Deerfield's overwhelming expectations is a credit to Boyden's inspirational leadership. The headmaster could not have realized his ambitions without them.

22

HORSES

If there is any one impression of Frank Boyden shared by all who knew him, it is the recollection of a small, stooped man driving a handsome Morgan horse. The headmaster enjoyed horses as much as he loved teaching boys. Horses were the greatest of Frank Boyden's few personal indulgences.

Despite the frenetic school schedule that occupied him from sun-up until midnight, Boyden rarely complained of fatigue. When he first publicly acknowledged "the strain" of managing "adolescents twenty four hours a day, seven days a week," the eighty-two-year-old headmaster cited horses as the secret to his tireless constitution. "If I can have a lively horse to drive for half an hour the tension seems to drain right out through my arms."

Boyden learned to love horses as a Foxboro youth. "You see, when I was a boy they thought it spoiled a good driving horse to ride him. So I never learned to ride. But I did learn to drive and I'll drive a horse as long as I am able." While in high school, Boyden's "chief ambition in life was to run a livery stable." After school he worked for his father driving visitors between the family foundry and the railroad station. After he was appointed Deerfield headmaster, Boyden arrived in town driving Pompey, a venerable Morgan his father gave him.

Boyden had a story for most every subject and horses were no exception. One of his favorite jokes described a Catholic chaplain assigned to a Protestant air squadron. "The chaplain got along wonderfully well with the boys," Boyden began. "They loved him and frequently sought his advice. One day three corpsmen approached him. 'Father,' they asked, 'Is it a sin to bet on a horse

race?' The chaplain looked at them a moment with a smile and said, 'Not if it's a fast horse.'"

Boyden was a fanatic about fast horses. Gravely afraid her husband would end his life in a buggy wreck, Helen Boyden didn't like horses "the least bit." But the headmaster insisted on "a horse with life." "When I go for a drive," he said, "I like to move." Boyden shared this interest in fast horses with Tom Murphy, whose child attended Deerfield. America's most celebrated harness driver, Murphy was familiarly known as the "Wizard of the Reigns." With career winnings totaling more than $1.5 million dollars, between 1909 and 1927 Murphy drove eleven of the twenty-nine trotters and pacers that finished a mile in two minutes or less.

When Murphy learned of Boyden's love for horses, he arrived in Deerfield with Talisman, the first of three world-class thoroughbreds he eventually gave the headmaster. "How they could go," Boyden whistled. "Those standard breds could really move!" Murphy became one of Boyden's dearest friends. "You are the person to whom I would quickly turn, in case anything serious developed here," Boyden wrote Murphy while hospitalized in 1962. "Your friendship and that of the family means more to us than is possible to express in words."

While many headmasters look forward each year to the first day of school, the day Boyden relished most was the running of the Hambletonian, harness racing's premier event. Much as Boyden enjoyed the race itself, his greatest thrill was keeping company with the eminent horseman Murphy. "One of the things which I always look forward to is the luncheon and dinner at his home in Poughkeepsie on the day of the Hambletonian Race," Boyden wrote a reporter in 1955. "It is a remarkable experience to go through the stands and about the stables and see the respect and admiration which people have for Mr. Murphy."

Although Boyden's love for horses transcended school politics and public relations, the headmaster, as always, capitalized on the practical advantages of his hobby. Speaking in New York at a celebration of his fiftieth year as headmaster, Boyden admitted "my strong liking for a horse and buggy is in this day and age an item of some news value." Writing to Murphy a decade later, Boyden

confessed, "I will be better known through my friendship with you and my interest in horses."

One loyal Boyden faculty member insists the headmaster's interest in horses was consciously calculated. "He didn't care a darn about horses," this forty-year schoolmaster said. "But those Rockefellers and other affluent New Yorkers . . . What did Mr. Boyden have to talk about with them? He couldn't talk about school. So he talked about horses." Horses did play a significant role in the evolution of Boyden's friendship with Henry Flynt, an association that made Deerfield's historic preservation possible. Deerfield also gained considerable media exposure in 1954, when President Dwight D. Eisenhower borrowed one of the headmaster's carriages to celebrate his first presidential birthday.

Boyden's personal interest in horses ran deeper than critics suggest. Self-effacing almost to the point of irritation, Boyden insisted, "I really don't know anything about horses except that I like them." But Boyden actually knew far more than he admitted. He conversed knowledgeably with Murphy about equine illness and proper shoeing technique and knew how to handle the feistiest horses right up to his final days.

Lewis Perry was convinced Boyden's intuitive ability to handle horses contributed directly to his knack for understanding students. Boyden later corroborated this appraisal when he equated Deerfield boys' need for athletics with a colt's need for exercise. Encouraging Deerfield seniors each year to "finish up strong," Boyden liked to use a horse racing analogy borrowed from Tom Murphy: "It is easier to make a record on a half-mile track," Boyden said, "because only a horse with real courage will not falter when he sees the long, last quarter mile ahead."

23

FAMILY

When asked to discuss his educational philosophy, Frank Boyden typically dismissed the question with a simple, direct response. "We just use the same pattern as in the family. We treat boys the same way as at home." This was a curious response from a man whose eldest son once described him as "not much of a father." Although Boyden maintained a boundless commitment to the Deerfield family, his own home life often suffered proportionately. This was a problem common to many headmasters' families.

Boyden's conviction about the relationship between family and school did not evolve from his own childhood. Boyden said little about his parents except that they were intensely religious and invariably short on cash. Helen Boyden suggested her husband's childhood wasn't entirely pleasant. "He'll tell you," she said. "He was brought up in a strict family. His father had a very unhumorous background. He was something of a Mr. Micawber. Every day something was going to happen."

Boyden did not seem to get along well with his brother Charles, who had difficulty finding steady work. Hoping to capitalize on his brother's growing reputation, Charles once proposed helping Frank operate Deerfield Academy and Dickinson High School for profit: "I believe we could take that school over and make a lot of money in case we could get along together. You know we look at a lot of things from different ways. If this point could be overcome and we could avoid friction, I would seriously consider it. Of course you could have charge of the boys and the school and I would plan to put my whole time in on the business end of the thing." Charles wanted to "run the place as a summer hotel or boarding house or possibly as

a summer school." But Frank was uninterested in collaboration. Deerfield Academy was his school alone.

It is most likely Boyden first appreciated the importance of extended family at Amherst, where he learned nearly everything else about running a school. A diffident introvert when he arrived, Boyden's personal growth in the supportive context of Amherst fraternity life, Charlie Garman's Saturday evening "bull" sessions, and President and Mrs. Harris's teas, receptions, and dinners was remarkable.

Boyden's marriage to Helen Childs was undoubtedly built on love and mutual interests. But it was also an advantageous professional match. Unlike other prep schools, where the headmaster's spouse often competed with the academy for her husband's attention, Deerfield benefitted from the Boydens' unique partnership. In many ways, Frank and Helen Boyden were cut from the same cloth. Both taught algebra, cherished small town Yankee values, and shared great faith in man's inherent goodness. Frank Boyden loved his wife. "I admire her for her gait if she be walking," he said quoting William Browne, a seventeenth century poet, "And for her wit if she be talking." Frank also cherished Helen because of her devotion to the school.

Beyond the academy, Frank and Helen Boyden had surprisingly little in common. "It is interesting the two of us could get together," Boyden said. Although the headmaster's greatest indulgence was horses, horses frightened Helen to death. Although Helen loved to travel abroad, the headmaster refused to board an airplane. "Helen of course is a very venturesome one," Boyden said. "Each time she gets an urge to go a long distance by some such means as an airplane, I settle back more and more firmly in the horse and buggy stage."

Playing bridge was one activity Helen and Frank Boyden shared, although they often played opposite each other with the headmaster typically getting the upper hand. "Mr. Boyden was a terrible bridge player," Van Miller recalled, "But his favorite suit was diamonds and he always seemed to come through with a successful diamond bid when the going got rough. I've forgotten just how we ended up in

the scoring, but I do remember that Mr. Boyden was the winner and he never ceased to gloat over it."

With limited time for their families while school was in session, many headmasters strived to make the most of vacations. Endicott Peabody of Groton is a good example. "F [Mrs. Peabody] and I see each other so little in term time," he said, "that I feel I ought not to leave her during the short breathing spaces we get on vacation."

The Boydens owned property on Lake Sunapee, where they tried to escape the term-time Deerfield grind. "It is important for my family to have a place to rally," the headmaster insisted. But appealing as the Sunapee retreat was in principle, the truth is Frank Boyden rarely allowed himself much leisure. Lewis Perry insisted Boyden "hates Lake Sunapee." More often than not, he arrived there in time for dinner and returned to Deerfield the same evening.

On the rare occasions Boyden set aside the burden of headmastering and devoted himself to family, he was an attentive parent and affectionate grandfather. "I am going up to Sunapee this weekend," he wrote Tom Murphy, "and just as soon as I change my clothes will go for a ride with Talisman. John's little boy, Cary, will probably be in bed when I arrive, but if he hears my voice will immediately ask if he can have a ride with Talisman Sunday morning. We tie a piece of clothesline about the length of a rein to the rings in the saddle and he holds on to that and imagines that he is driving himself."

But Boyden was most often obsessed with Deerfield. Although Helen Boyden accepted her husband's compulsion which she shared in many ways herself, the Boyden children sometimes begrudged their second-rate status. The eldest of three siblings, John Boyden worked with his father for thirty-five years as head of the day student department and director of admissions. John had little recollection of Boyden as family man. "I've known the Headmaster intimately in two ways, as my headmaster and as my employer. I was scared of him." John considered Boyden "the most selfish man I ever knew."

Likewise, when Boyden's daughter Betty was born, Deerfield lore insists the headmaster's first words to his still anesthetized wife were about the academy. "What are we going to do about Ben Stebbins?" Boyden asked. "He's such a fool." Betty later described her father

as a "fibber," a fitting description for a man who publicly championed the importance of family but privately neglected his own. Helen Boyden shared this estimation. "For an absolutely truthful man," she said, "he is the biggest liar I have ever known."

As far as the Deerfield family was concerned, Helen was the headmaster's "helpmate, soulmate, companion and colleague." But in their own home, the Boydens' relationship was more strained. "He'll be angry in the house," Helen said, "then go out and be sweet with the faculty and the boys. His father was just like that. Gracious to other people, but how he yips at his family. He makes his boys be neat, but around here he throws everything on the floor. I spend half my time looking for the things he loses. Why do I always do what he tells me to do?"

Helen agreed with her husband because, to a great extent, she shared his ambitions for Deerfield. In fact, having grown up in town, Helen Boyden may have had a greater personal stake in the academy's fortunes than the headmaster. Boyden sometimes complained that he would have been a lawyer or politician were it not for his wife. It was Helen who bound Boyden to Deerfield. It was Deerfield, in turn, that solidified and validated the Boydens' marriage.

24

MRS. BOYDEN

In 1934 Smith College conferred an honorary doctorate on "Helen Childs Boyden, sound scientist and brilliant teacher, who with some slight assistance from her husband created in Deerfield Academy one of the truly great schools in the country." Frank Boyden liked to joke about this citation but he knew it was quite true.

Unlike the headmaster, who concentrated on schoolwide tasks, Mrs. Boyden was before all else a classroom teacher. Where Boyden instructed Deerfield students through school meetings, athletics, family-style meals and private conversations, his wife taught them each day, chalk in hand, lesson by lesson. "I count Mrs. Boyden among the few great teachers I have ever had," said Victor Butterfield '22, former president of Wesleyan University. "She embodies, as do very few, the total wealth of qualities which make cultivated living an inspired thing. She gives the life of the mind a dignity, a depth, and a range which command the respect of all."

While the headmaster emphasized proper conduct and character, Helen Boyden focused more on precise thinking and problem solving. As Deerfield's ablest teacher, she represented the most convincing counterpoint to those who criticized Deerfield's relative indifference to topnotch academics. "Mrs. Boyden undoubtedly has set the intellectual tone of the School," Butterfield said. "Because of the soundness of her intellectual concerns and the intensity with which she seeks the truth, the modesty with which she pursues and reveals it and the beautiful blend of tolerance and conviction which she reveals, the academic life of the school has been extremely healthy."

Helen Childs joined the Deerfield faculty in 1905, after distinguishing herself in the natural sciences at Greenfield High School and Smith. Her interest in this discipline was unusual

considering the scarcity of women scientists at the turn of the century. Together with her mentor, Jenny Sheldon, Helen Boyden played a crucial role in integrating science into the Deerfield curriculum.

Like Sheldon, Helen Boyden had poor eyesight, an infirmity that required her to identify students by assigned seats. Returning to Deerfield each June for reunions, alumni were often astounded at her ability to recall their former seat assignment. Nearly a decade after his graduation Jerry Angell was shocked when she greeted him warmly as "the blue coated boy in the second seat from the left in the third row."

Sheldon and Boyden also shared a preference for encouraging independent thinking rather than rote memorization. "Our greatest difficulty is to make the young observe and observe accurately," Sheldon wrote. "The general complaint is that the students do not see things as they are or think about them inductively." Helen Boyden likewise implored Deerfield students to "stop trying to remember and start trying to think."

Although she took the sciences seriously, Helen Boyden also excited students' general interest in studying while concurrently introducing them to broad ethical concepts. "She loves learning for its own sake," said Butterfield, "but knows too of its immediate and vital bearing on wisdom and living."

Helen Boyden's classes, by her own recollection, "followed the romance of hydrogen and oxygen . . . thrilled to the logic of the remainder theorem and the beauty of the elliptic curve . . . and traced the tiny atom Dalton as it changed to a whirling universe and ended in the magnificent climax of the atomic bomb."

Boyden's lessons also included "Whatever came to mind," according to Peter Atkinson '62. "It might be baseball, the passing of her dear Boston Braves. Or politics. Or she'd talk about the school in its early days. Like this, Mrs. Boyden made algebra an all inclusive subject, drawing us on by interweaving with it all her fascination and delight in the whole vast world."

Although Helen Boyden taught science and math, she was beloved for encouraging creative thinking and building self-confidence. "Make up your mind what you want in life," she said. "Be sure it is

worthy; be willing to pay the price; and go get it." A familiar sign posted on her bulletin board read, "The difficult we do immediately. The impossible will take a little longer."

No Boyden class began without a favorite aphorism etched on the blackboard. Helen Boyden's favorite, "Other fools have learned it, so can I," reflects her inimitable modesty and sense of humor. Other memorable Boydenisms include:

The trouble you don't get into, you don't have to get out of.
The man who is too big for a small job is too small for a big job.
Choose a high failure rather than a low success.
You always have to sacrifice something little for something big.

Helen Boyden was at her best with weak and diffident students. "At fifteen, when I first met her," Waldo Sessions '27 recalls, "she seemed a bit austere and stern. But the first time I was in one of her classes I felt a warmth and understanding that ultimately contributed to changing many conceptions I had of life. She and she alone taught me how to study. And this is from a boy whom the Headmaster once said, 'Waldo doesn't break the rules around here; he simply rises above them.'"

"You had the confidence in me that I didn't have in myself," Steve Warck added. "You tried very hard to teach me that all I needed was belief in myself to accomplish what ever I wished to accomplish. It was a lesson that has served me well in later years. Even on those occasions when I have fallen short."

The depths of Helen Boyden's patience with students were unfathomable. Chandler Kellers remembers Mrs. Boyden "catching me reading *College Humor* in algebra class, then later helping me with extra tutoring in the same subject. I still have trouble balancing my checkbook and probably couldn't pass your easiest chemistry exam. But I know I'll never forget some of the basic things about life I learned from you at Deerfield in and out of class."

Like the headmaster, Helen Boyden relied on a well-stocked pedagogical arsenal to motivate even the most reluctant students. "She used all her delightfully underhanded tricks on us," Atkinson

said, "flattery, disappointed faith in us, 'what would the headmaster say if he knew,' the weak-and-feeble-woman-act, out-and-out cajolery . . . everything except tears which, she says, she reserves for the headmaster."

Warck described the "unconscionable lengths" Mrs. Boyden went to get her lesson across. "I can still remember a 95 grade on a chemistry quiz when my correct mark was 55. When I pointed out your error, you airily dismissed it with the remark that I 'would get a 95 next time.' So, of course, after that, I couldn't fail you or myself in legitimately getting a 95 'the next time.'"

As a full-time classroom teacher, Helen Boyden was unique among headmaster's wives. While many spouses toiled anonymously in their husband's shadow, Helen Boyden took a prominent role by the headmaster's side. To his credit, Frank Boyden encouraged his wife and did his best to acknowledge her professional contributions. "Speaking now only as a headmaster," Boyden wrote a *Newsweek* editor, "may I say that she is really one of the truly great teachers, helping and guiding boys not only in the classroom but helping them establish a way of life."

The headmaster valued his wife's work not only because she was good at it but because it allowed him to reallocate his own efforts elsewhere. As Boyden's emphasis shifted from teaching boys to building buildings in the 1950s, his schedule required more work on administrative and development tasks. Forced to spend much time away from the boys, Boyden's appreciation of Helen's work grew proportionately. "I was pleased with the reference to Mrs. Boyden," he wrote *Newsweek* in 1957, "Her interest in the lives of thousands of boys is a far greater one than my own." With his wife ably manning the front lines, Boyden himself was freed to concentrate more on admissions, development, and other trustee issues requisite for building a nationally recognized academy.

Although she was a distinguished instructor with a heavy five-course load, Helen Boyden was not excused from any of the responsibilities expected of headmasters' wives who did not teach. On a typical school day, she awoke at dawn to work in her greenhouse, read, and prepare breakfast. She next taught her five classes, which concluded at 2:00, offered extra-help between 2:00 and 3:00, attended

home athletic contests in the afternoon, served a family-style dinner to faculty and students thereafter, then retired to her living room where she hosted faculty coffee. More students arrived in the evening seeking tutoring, cookies, or consolation. And a handful of her husband's administrative "lieutenants" were sure to gather in the parlor after the boys were bedded down around 10:30. In addition, trustees and other invited and impromptu visitors stayed overnight with the Boydens at the headmaster's insistence.

If Deerfield was the extended family Boyden envisioned, Helen Boyden was Deerfield's school mother. Stitching torn clothing, comforting homesick boys, and tending to the ill and the injured weighed heavily on her regular agenda, as did supporting Deerfield athletics. This was especially true during baseball season, when Mrs. Boyden served as the varsity team's official scorer. "Her thick, well-kept scorebook is testimony of the wins and losses she has shared with them," the *Scroll* reported. "At every home game, she sits on the third base bleachers and, using the eyes of the coterie of faculty wives and boys about her, she accurately scores every play. Her vision doesn't carry much past the home team bench ten yards in front, but her understanding of boys and baseball bound her closely to every game. Win or lose, three seasons a year, through soccer, football, swimming, track and basketball and hockey, she is in the stands, watching 'her boys.' The teacher of the classroom is the spectator of the games, part of everything."

Described by one educational historian as "aggressively male oases in an increasingly feminized American culture," boys' boarding schools like Deerfield tended to reinforce traditional patriarchal and authoritarian attitudes. This certainly was not a comfortable environment for women, which explains the preponderance of bachelor schoolmasters. Few prep school women endured it at all. Fewer still achieved the monumental presence Helen Boyden did.

For many Deerfield boys, Helen Boyden personified the feminine ideal, the lone voice of compassion and understanding in a competitive macho milieu. As one former student said, "Mrs. Boyden is the finest woman I have ever met. She has humility, tolerance, humor, Godliness, and all the other abstract qualities which we think of as noble." When a Deerfield alumnus told his bride he

had always hoped to marry a woman like Mrs. Boyden, the newlywed woman wrote the headmaster's wife, "I hope I am able to come close to Dan's hopes." This bride's diffidence is understandable, since it is doubtful Helen Boyden's Deerfield record of achievements will ever be surpassed.

As her honorary degree from Mount Holyoke College attests, Helen Childs Boyden's lifetime accomplishments seem well beyond reach of any one individual. "Friend, consoler and counselor, foster mother, mentor, hostess, and guiding star: the range of your roles seems a composite of all women rather than one woman."

When Helen Boyden died in 1973 after a sixty-three-year teaching career, the Greenfield *Recorder* observed, "It is not likely that Frank L. Boyden could have achieved so many goals without the aid of Helen Childs. Together, the Boydens created not only a great institution, but brought into Deerfield the spirit and endearment that have given the entire village permanence. Mrs. Boyden was a great teacher, a singularly remarkable benefactor for thousands of young men, and a beloved woman. Her spirit helped build Deerfield Academy and will remain with it forever."

"Lest you think Helen Boyden will be remembered only as the wife of a great man," Congressman Silvio Conte warned, "this woman stood in no man's shadow. It would be hard to imagine a woman more respected by more people."

25

PUBLIC EDUCATION

Although he had transformed Deerfield's public high school into an exclusive independent academy, Frank Boyden remained committed to preparing all American youth for patriotic and productive American citizenship. Boyden criticized educators who tried to differentiate between public and private schools. "It is a foolish argument," he insisted. "There is so much more to be done than both can do."

Throughout his life, Boyden was actively involved in public service. Presidents Franklin D. Roosevelt and Harry S Truman recognized Boyden's broad educational vision and civic commitment by appointing him to the National Youth Administration and the Navy Civilian Advisory Committee. On the state level, Boyden engineered the University of Massachusetts's transition from a small agricultural college to a nationally recognized public university.

When Franklin D. Roosevelt assumed the presidency in 1933, the United States economy was mired in unimaginable depression, while the world's democratic nations braced for likely confrontation with totalitarian regimes. More than twelve million Americans were unemployed. Five thousand banks had failed. Farm prices had fallen to their lowest point in history. With poor prospects for self-improvement, the public mood was grim. Democracy itself seemed in jeopardy. To provide immediate relief and initiate long-overdue reform, Roosevelt initiated the New Deal to restore American hope and confidence in individual and national progress.

Roosevelt, like Boyden, was troubled by the economic circumstances impeding the education and development of

American youth. The Depression had hit children hardest. Employers hired unemployed adults for positions once staffed by young men and women. Children dropped out of high school in greater numbers. Without work to provide wages that paid tuition, college was out of the question for most students. Many leaders feared these circumstances were alienating youth, who were the future strength of American democracy.

In 1935 Roosevelt appointed Boyden to the Advisory Committee of the National Youth Administration (NYA). "The problem of assisting in the adjustment of Youth under existing conditions is one of the most important problems that confront us," Roosevelt wrote Boyden. "I feel that you are particularly well-equipped to give us valuable counsel." Boyden's eight-year NYA appointment complemented his lifelong interest in training American youth for civic involvement. According to S. Burns Weston, an Ohio NYA officer, the program's first priority was "to provide immediate constructive outlets for the energy and hope that was frustrated by idleness." Boyden concurred with Weston, who believed "no form of government will last which denies to a substantial number of young men and women the opportunity to assume their normal place in the working world." As an NYA advisor, Boyden helped develop, organize, and supervise over 12,000 federal, state, and local committees dedicated to improving the education, health, recreation, and employment prospects of American youth.

In 1946 the Truman administration followed Roosevelt's lead by appointing Boyden to the Navy Civilian Advisory Committee. Following World War II the armed forces faced problems with demobilization, volunteer recruitment, and preparation and training for the impending cold war. In a March letter to Boyden, Secretary of the Navy James F. Forrestal and Fleet Admiral Chester Nimitz sought advice "whereby the life of the men in naval service will be made interesting, instructive, and attractive as possible." The Civilian Advisory Committee would recommend suggestions to improve "Navy morale and welfare, education of reserves, and preparation for return to civilian life."

Forrestal also requested comment "on naval policies, and practices which are misunderstood or disapproved by the public."

On 26 April Boyden joined members of the committee that included Supreme Court Justice William O. Douglas on board the aircraft carrier *USS Tarawa* in Gravesend Bay, New York. James J. McConaughy, the committee chairman and former president of Wesleyan University, focused the group on issues that had occupied Frank Boyden for nearly fifty years: "Your concern is with the boy who serves in a peacetime Navy. How can 18 months, 3 years, or more, of service be made more valuable to him as a citizen? Can his parents have greater confidence that their boy is rendering significant service to his country, that if he returns to civilian life he will be a wiser, stronger, and more useful citizen because of his Navy experience? Could the boy during his period of Navy service receive sufficient general training so that, when his enlistment is over, he would have gained the equivalent of a year of general schooling, or a semester of college?"

When this meeting adjourned, Boyden donned cold-weather gear and climbed to the flight deck to observe training maneuvers of Air Group Four. In an awesome display of naval firepower, seventy-five F4U Corsairs, TBF Avengers, and SB2C Helldivers were launched by catapult from the *Tarawa*'s deck. Once airborne, the planes bombed, shelled, and strafed a target towed behind the ship. After the demonstration Boyden fell in with enlisted men and ate lunch in the crew's mess quarters. In later years, Boyden remembered this day as "one of the most thrilling experiences of my life."

As one of five members on the education and training subcommittee, Boyden's recommendations contributed to development and implementation of the Naval Reserve Officers Training Corps and the Naval Aviation College Program. Both programs financed education and training of junior naval officers and a reserve of trained officers prepared to serve in national emergencies. These programs were among the most creative and remarkable educational opportunities ever offered American youth.

During World War II and throughout the cold war and baby boom, Frank Boyden's services were in similar demand on the state level. In 1942 Massachusetts Governor Leverett Saltonstall appointed Boyden to the Massachusetts State College board of trustees. With most American youth in uniform, college enrollment remained small. The school had only 1,500 students and a $ 1 million dollar budget. But peace and the GI Bill brought students back to school in unprecedented numbers. In 1947 the college reorganized as the University of Massachusetts and launched an ambitious building program. It also revised its curriculum to meet the heightened technological and professional expectations of the *Sputnik* era.

The University of Massachusetts's dramatic growth was not without problems. As the Massachusetts legislature appropriated more money for higher education, it demanded greater authority to control its expenditure. Throughout the 1950s university trustees battled legislators over the school's budget. They also challenged the legislature's insistence on authorizing appointments and salaries of all professional staff. This bitter debate provoked President Jean Paul Mather's resignation in 1959, after the Massachusetts Senate denied fiscal independence for the university.

With Boyden now appointed board chairman, the University of Massachusetts (UMass) faced a crucial test. "It seems clear," said Richard Glenn Gettell, a UMass Trustee and President of Mount Holyoke College, "that the university is at a fork in the road: either it will move forward to become a major state university, or it will slide backwards and be a large but mediocre institution." Appointing a new president was Boyden's immediate priority. But given the political context of Mather's resignation, this would not be an easy task. Charles W. Cole, another UMass trustee and president of Amherst College believed "nobody but a very stupid or inexperienced man (whom we would not want) would take the job." Boyden was not discouraged. He personally delivered the university's concerns to the Massachusetts legislature, where he had lobbied for public and private education since 1917. He intended to secure the

university's fiscal and administrative independence as he had done years before at Deerfield Academy and Dickinson High School.

"In some sections of Vermont they still farm in the old way," Boyden told a group assembled to recommend a university president and support new legislation advocating fiscal autonomy. "Instead of baling hay, they pile it in haycocks and load it by pitchfork. It always was and still is, a difficult and real art to lay a load securely Education today has been under many heavy loads. But if we all get our pitchforks and work together, we can solve many problems. Massachusetts long has led in education. We have the faculty. We have the students and the equipment. We need an outstanding leader. We need your help."

Against great odds, Boyden secured the contentious fiscal autonomy bill and persuaded John Lederle to accept the UMass presidency. Lederle considered this bill "the single most important legislation" in the university's history. Before resigning from the UMass board in 1969, after more than twenty-five years of service, Boyden helped establish the UMass medical school and the UMass-Boston campus. He also upgraded the university athletic programs, including construction of the Frank L. Boyden Gymnasium, a familiar milepost to all who approach UMass from the south.

Under Boyden's direction, the university's enrollment doubled from ten thousand to twenty thousand while its budget increased from $ 10 million to $ 41 million. President Lederle described Boyden's contribution to the University of Massachusetts as "an almost unparalleled record of achievement in American higher education under the Board Chairmanship of one man." When Frank Boyden died at age ninety-two in May 1972, Alexander Brin, former chairman of the Massachusetts Board of Education, said, "The public school system of the nation has had no better or more consistent friend."

26

LEADER

When Frank Boyden ended his Deerfield tenure in 1968, he was hailed as "the uncontested dean of independent school headmasters, the last of a breed of one school men and one man schools." When Boyden died four years later, at age ninety-three, he was praised as "a towering figure in the world of education and in the very lives of all of those he touched." Boyden's example reaffirmed essential truths and ideals. His achievement inspired others to pursue dreams and ambitions of their own.

Boyden's skill as a leader began with precise recognition of his own strengths and weaknesses. A product of turn-of-the-century progressive America, Boyden dedicated his life to the values he learned in his youth. Although he entertained numerous offers for more prestigious and profitable appointments, Boyden chose to remain a schoolmaster, the endeavor for which he was best suited. On one occasion, Boyden and Lewis Perry discussed a faculty member who had left Deerfield to pursue misplaced aspirations in higher education. "Ambition is a good thing," Perry wrote, "but it often leads people astray." Boyden concurred. "I agree with your diagnosis. How fortunate that we both have kept within our abilities."

Although he might have worked as field secretary for Teddy Roosevelt's American Playground and Recreation Commission or moved to the nation's capital to pursue political fortunes, as did his friend Speaker of the House John McCormack, Boyden opted to remain a career educator. Running a school was what Boyden did best, a fact he was astute enough to recognize and respect. "Frank Boyden was a man perfectly fit for the position he was in," the Reverend William Park said, "and somehow or another he knew it."

Boyden's self-knowledge was essential to his professional success as one of his favorite poems attests:

> When you get what you want in your struggle for pelf,
> And the world makes you King for a day,
> Then go to the mirror and look at yourself,
> And see what that guy has to say.
>
> You can fool the whole world down the pathway of years,
> And get pats on the back as you pass,
> But your final reward will be heartaches and tears,
> If you've cheated the guy in the glass.

Boyden recognized the vital relationship between quality education and quality living. He feared contemporary society was eroding personal relationships and community identity. As the world entered the nuclear age, Boyden's fears multiplied. "Human history becomes more and more a race between education and catastrophe," the headmaster said, quoting H.G. Wells.

At Deerfield, Boyden crafted an ideal model of individual and community life. He believed quality living in an imperfect world depended upon values nurtured in youth. Boyden agreed with Al Stearns on this subject. "Youth has still its God-given visions of what life can and should be," Stearns wrote. "Only as it realizes these visions in its later years will it find life rich and full and free; and experience teaches us only too plainly that youth must have the help of its elders if it is to reach the high goal that these visions challenge it to seek."

As Deerfield alumni attest, Frank Boyden had a remarkable gift for communicating his vision by word and by example. "Deerfield has given me a sense of joy and fullness of life in the midst of a world that is confused and torn," said Stephen Rockefeller '54. "It has taught me to put my heart into life whether in studies or athletics, work or play. It has shown me a community where each person is responsible to participate. It has strengthened and humbled me with lessons of defeat. But heartened me also by showing me I could win. It has imparted to me something fine and good, something healthy

and strong. And it has taught me to respect it and live according to it."

Boyden knew who he was, what he wanted, and why he wanted it. Boyden developed his own definition of leadership and communicated it directly to Deerfield faculty in these eleven "Requisites of a Teacher":

1. Sincere interest in and full knowledge of his subject
2. Ability to make subject interesting to others
3. Ability to link own subject with other important fields
4. Sense of humor
5. Understanding of and sympathy with problems of youth
6. Self-control and ability to control others
7. Personality
8. A mind receptive to new ideas
9. A hobby
10. An optimistic philosophy of life
11. Ability to select important points

These expectations for others were consistent with those Boyden set for himself. His words invariably agreed with his deeds. One of Boyden's greatest leadership strengths was his reliable consistency, respect, and support.

Boyden knew himself well and had an uncanny knack for understanding others. Boyden also recognized the difficulty of making dreams come true. From his first battle with P. D. Bridges, Boyden demonstrated unusual ability in linking his educational vision with the political and organizational strategies necessary to achieve it. While many headmasters preferred the isolation of their rural academies, Boyden plunged headfirst into the whirl of American politics and finance. By forging critical connections with presidents, senators, congressmen, and businessmen, Boyden built one of the finest secondary schools in the nation, while pioneering greater long-term collaboration between American educators and capitalists.

No assessment of Boyden as leader can ignore his longevity. Boyden's sixty-six-year tenure is a credit to his imagination, flexibility, and physical health. While the ideals Boyden espoused

were essentially timeless, Boyden's specific expression of those ideals varied to meet the changing needs of the school, the local community, and the nation.

In 1951 Charlie Merrill applauded his friend's insistence on continuously reinventing himself and his school. "I realize it is asking too much to request you to relax. I know how anxious you are to get every dream fulfilled. I also realize that as soon as the present dream comes to fulfillment, you will dream up something else again." Merrill reminded Boyden that "Deerfield will never be completed in your lifetime or in mine."

Significant as Boyden's life's work was, the headmaster's most enduring achievement was building a physical and moral foundation for future generations. In his final year at Deerfield, Boyden himself agreed, "A school gains its character from all the people who once came to study and play and live there, and from the traditions which have grown from its past and become part of its present. But no educational institution can afford to live in the past or simply in the present."

In the end, a leader's vision either endures or fades. The persistence of a leader's ideals in his absence is a principal index of superior leadership. Although a leader's work speaks best for itself and words are often forgotten, Frank Boyden chose to be remembered by this selection from Tennyson's *Ulysses*:

> Come my friends,
> 'Tis not too late to seek a newer world
> Tho' much is taken, much abides; and tho'
> We are not now that strength which in old days
> Moved earth and heaven; that which we are, we are;
> One equal temper of heroic hearts,
> Made weak by time and fate, but strong in will
> To strive, to seek, to find, and not to yield.

ACKNOWLEDGEMENTS

This biography began in the spring of 1987, when I first visited the Deerfield Academy archives at the Frank L. Boyden Library. After teaching at Deerfield for a year, I had grown curious about Frank Boyden, who was universally lionized by school legends but often forgotten in fact. Like many who are familiar with Frank Boyden and with Deerfield, my own impression of Boyden was largely informed by John McPhee's colorful biographical sketch, *The Headmaster*. Although appreciative of Mr. McPhee's acclaimed work, I was unsatisfied with it as the sole published interpretation of Frank Boyden's extraordinary life. In 1992, when I struggled to find a publisher for this book, Mr. McPhee's support corroborated my belief that this new rendering is justified.

When this book was just an idea, Tina Cohen and Jim Marksbury at Deerfield Academy and Donald Friary at Historic Deerfield shared my conviction that it was a worthy project. Throughout my research, Tina Cohen was a welcome guide to the expansive records of Boyden's tenure, most of which had never before been studied. I am especially grateful for Tina's good humor, thoughtfulness, integrity and professional skills. More than anyone else at Deerfield Academy, Jim Marksbury recognized the merit of a balanced, honest assessment of Frank Boyden's work. By publishing my earliest articles on Tom Ashley and Mrs. Boyden in *Deerfield* magazine and by offering ongoing encouragement, Jim introduced my work to academy alumnae/i and friends. Together, Tina and Jim selected the photographs that contribute immeasurably to this book. A historian and executive director of Historic Deerfield, Inc., Donald Friary read early draft manuscripts, challenged my preliminary interpretations, asked incisive questions, and recommended revisions and additional research that contributed to the book's historical integrity. More recently, Donald was a helpful advocate for this book's publication.

To the many librarians, archivists, staff, and specialists who assisted me at the Frank L. Boyden Library, the Pocumtuck Valley Memorial and Historic Deerfield libraries, the Foxboro Public Library, the Amherst College Archives, the Smith College Library, the University of Massachusetts Library, the Loyola Marymount University Library, and the Harvard University libraries, thank you. Your many contributions are written onto each page of this book.

Although I completed most of my research while teaching at Deerfield Academy, much of this book was written while studying at the Harvard Graduate School of Education. At that time, when my financial resources were scarce, thoughtful gifts from Bob and Ellen Kaufmann, Jim Schoff, Jim Stevens, Gates Hawn, Phil Weymouth, Jr., and Fred and Sheila Rockwell helped support and advance the book toward publication. Equally important, Rick Melvoin offered invaluable support and personal perspective on writing and publishing a historical book.

As the manuscript evolved through early drafts, constructive comments from Peter Smith and William Sheldon Howe improved it considerably. Doug Wilson, editor of *Amherst* magazine, assisted with the chapter on Boyden's Amherst College years. Joe Medlicott offered ongoing general comments and suggestions that cheered me and improved my writing. While the book benefitted greatly from these and other historical and editorial suggestions, any errors of fact or interpretation are mine alone.

No book gets to print without significant word-processing and related technical efforts. John Smith at Santa Fe Community College helped me reformat my manuscript from Macintosh to IBM WordPerfect. Several anonymous computer specialists at Loyola Marymount University similarly reformatted an early draft from TeachText into Macintosh. I am generally appreciative for the word-processing and duplicating resources made available to me by Johns Hopkins University Center for Talented Youth, Harvard University, Loyola Marymount University, and Santa Fe Community College.

Securing a publisher was perhaps the most challenging aspect of this book. At a time when I was failing independently, Jim Banner provided vital encouragement and useful suggestions. Without Jim's enthusiastic assistance, the manuscript might have ended up in a box

on a dusty shelf. I am thankful to Michael Perry at Deerfield Academy for introducing me to Jim and for Michael's own quiet but significant support.

To Jed Lyons and Julie Kirsch at Madison Books and University Press of America, Inc. who recognized this book's merit and agreed to publish it for readers beyond Deerfield Academy's alumnae/i and friends, thank you. For assistance with design and production, I am indebted to Gisele Marie Byrd, Jennifer Ruark, and Melissa McNitt.

To the teachers who shaped my understanding of history, education and leadership, Oscar Handlin, Stanley Hoffmann, Nathan Glazer, Joel Perlmann, Rob Laubacher, Lee Bolman, Kent Chabotar, Jay Heubert, and Bob Gilpin, my deepest respect and appreciation. To the teachers who taught me to write a passable sentence, Guy Hughes, John Charles Smith, and Chuck Burdick, thank you.

For teaching me the importance of schools and the power of books and for dedicating much of their lives to educating me, I thank my mother, Dorothy Ann Cooke, and my father, John Joseph Cooke.

And with all my heart I thank my wife Monica Silveira Cyrino, who daily teaches, inspires and reminds me "what is precious."

—— *Brian Cooke*

NOTES

Abbreviations

AC Amherst College Archives and Special Collections
DA Deerfield Academy Archives and Special Collections
FLB Frank Learoyd Boyden
HD Historic Deerfield and Pocumtuck Valley Memorial Association Libraries
SC Smith College Archives and Special Collections
UM University of Massachusetts Archives

1. "A LITTLE BUG"

1 Boyden and Maynard at Amherst commencement: John Henry Frizzell, "Frank L. Boyden Headmaster Extraordinaire." *The Shield of Phi Kappa Psi*, Summer 1967 (AC).
1 Bethany Sunday School picnic: *Foxboro Reporter*, 9 August 1902.
1 Athletics to play Sharon: *Foxboro Reporter*, 9 August 1902.
1 FLB receives two letters: The *Boston Globe*, 14 January 1965.
2 Foxboro defeats Sharon: *Foxboro Reporter*, 16 August 1902.
2 Dissatisfaction with trustees: *Springfield Republican*, 6 May 1900.
2 A headmaster or an undertaker: McPhee, *The Headmaster*, p. 5.
2 FLB accepts appointment: FLB to B. Stebbins, Jr., 12 August 1902 (DA).

2. FOXBORO

3 FLB reads hometown news: FLB to Sullivan, 21 March 1947 (DA).
3 FLB emphasizes Foxboro values: FLB to Philip Bourne, 25 January 1943 (DA).
3 Foxboro named after Charles James Fox: Authelet, p. 3.
3 FLB helps found Historical Society: Lane, pp. 148-149.
3 Foxboro's public buildings: Lane, p. 157.
4 FLB's parents teach: FLB to Mrs. Samuel Hammond, 16 June 1949 (DA); FLB to Mrs. G. S. Torrey, 17 March 1967 (DA).
4 Benjamin Boyden: *History and Directory of Foxboro 1890*.
4 Anna Boyden: McPhee, p. 3.

4 Otis Cary: unattributed biography most likely composed by one of FLB's uncles (DA).

4 FLB attends Cary School: FLB to George Hamp, 27 January 1967 (DA).

5 Political clubs: Lane, p. 141.

5 Temperance: Lane, p. 167.

5 Church: Lane, p. 142.

5 Van Choate Electric: *Foxboro Reporter*, 20 April 1894, 15 June 1894, 13 May 1898, 2 February 1900.

6 Small town mystic qualities: Lane, p. 141.

6 FLB's philosophy, a code of that era: McPhee, p. 33.

6 Barton family: Lane, p. 130.

6 FLB recalls Barton family: FLB to Alfred Young, 22 February 1955 (DA).

6 FLB quotes Lincoln: FLB Personal, Talks File (DA).

6 Barton's speech on heritage: *Foxboro Sesquicentennial Booklet*.

6 FLB's high school commencment: *Foxboro Reporter*, 27 June 1896.

7 Tutors for Amherst admission: FLB to Mrs. G. S. Torrey, 17 March 1967 (DA).

3. AMHERST

9 Garman describes a college man's world: Garman to Mr. Keith '02,

9 28 January 1903, Box XXIV Garman Papers (AC).

9 "So green, so small, so scared": McPhee, pp. 37, 38.

9 "a midnight oil burner": McPhee, p. 38.

9 "a cipher": McPhee, p. 38.

9 "waifs and strays": *The Shield of Phi Kappa Psi*, Summer 1967.

9 Bigelow and Patton remember Amherst: Claude Moore Fuess, *Amherst: The Story of A New England College*, 1935.

10 George Harris was not an intellectual: Thomas Le Duc, *Intellect and Piety at Amherst College*, p. 138.

10 FLB quotes Pinchot: FLB Personal,Talks (DA).

10 Mrs. Harris on etiqutte: Fuess.

11 Eliot praises Amherst physical education: Fuess.

11 Edward Hitchcock: Fuess.

11 George Olds: Fuess.

12 FLB/Olds correspondence: FLB to Olds, December 1926; Olds to FLB 16 December 1926 FLB Papers Vox VII, 16 (AC).

12 Keedy recognizes Garman: "Grove Oration," *The Amherst Student*, Commencement Issue 1902 (AC).

13 Jack Frizzell on Garman: Frizzell to Amherst Class of 1902, 2 June 1967 (AC).

13 Garman's emphasis on public stewardship: Preserved Smith '01 quoted in *Amherst Graduate Quarterly*, November 1937 (AC).

14 Maynard, Wilson, and Trevoy Biography: Amherst College Bio Files, Class of 1902 (AC); Deerfield Academy Trustee Files (DA).

15 Anson Morse defines success: Frizzell to Class of 1902, 2 June 1967 (AC).

4. REVIVAL

17 Frightening youths: McPhee, p. 4, p. 14; Frederick Stebbins '16 letter to *Scroll* 1962 for FLB's 60th anniversary at Deerfield (DA).

17 Sibley wrote FLB: R. W. Sibley to FLB, August 1902 (DA).

17 Details of Deerfield politics: *Springfield Republican*, 6 May 1900.

20 Andrew Campbell: Deerfield Academy Trustee Files (DA).

20 FLB on Campbell: FLB to Rev. Osmond J. Billings, 3 June 1925; FLB to Mrs. Andrew Campbell, 30 October 1946 (DA).

21 "Bossism has been overthrown": *Springfield Republican*, 6 May 1900.

21 FLB quotes Lincoln: FLB Personal, Talks (DA).

21 Dumont Lamb: 1904 Class History, Valedictory, Class Will (DA).

21 "Develop the scholars physically and morally": *Greenfield Gazette and Courier*, 18 June 1903.

23 DADHS 25th Anniversary: *Greenfield Gazette*, 17 June 1903; Program for 25th Anniversary, 12 June 1903 (DA).

5. COMMUNITY CENTER

25 "My faith in teenagers": FLB Speech to Chappaqua PTA c. 1951 in FLB Personal, Talks (DA).

25 "I believe in the home": Chappaqua Speech (DA).

26 Boyden challenged students: FLB Speech to American Playground Recreation Commission, 7 May 1913 in FLB Personal, Talks (DA).

26 Students meet FLB's challenge: Dumont Lamb, Class of 1904 History, Valedictory, Class Will (DA).

26 Letter from Connecticut boy: FLB Talks (DA).

26 FLB on athletics, parties and drama: Recreation Speech (DA).

6. LOCAL POLITICS

29 FLB to Goodell: 2 August 1948 (DA).

30 Enrollment and bank failure: 1908 Deerfield School Committee Report (DA).

30 Greenough's business: FLB Talks (DA).

30 Greenough biography: Trustee File (DA).

31 Greenough/Bridges arguments: *Deerfield School Committee Reports 1903-4* (DA).

7. HELEN CHILDS

33 At Greenfield High: *Greenfield Gazette and Courier*, 30 June 1900 (DA).

33 At Smith: *Smith College 1904 Yearbook* (SC).

34 Intellectual womanliness: Charlotte Burgis DeForest, *An Undergraduate View of Smith College 1875-1908* (AC)

34 No physical beauty: *Greenfield Recorder*, 20 September 1963.

34 Looked like Eleanor Roosevelt: Alvin F. Dickle, "Goodbye Mr. Chips" in *Greenfield Recorder* undated c. 1968 (DA).

34 Wedding: Newspaper clippings 50th anniversary 1957 (DA).

35 "a conspiracy for the good": Michael Platt to Doug Gortner, 1987 (DA).

35 Deerfield note to bridegroom: *Deerfield Alumni Journal*, Spring 1972 (DA).

8. WORKING TOGETHER

37 Recruiting students: American Playground Recreation Speech, 1913 (DA).

38 A raft to cross river: Lena and Ada '13, 1962 letters (DA).

38 Manual training: Recreation Speech 1913 (DA).

39 Girls could keep ahead of boys: *Pemawachuatuck*, June 1912 (DA).

40 Singing: Mary Eddy '06, 1962 letters (DA).

40 *Boston Globe* report: 22 March 1908.

9. TOM ASHLEY

41 In Boyden's words: FLB quoted in Amelia F. Miller, "Thomas Williams Ashley" in *Deerfield Alumni Journal*, Autumn 1962 (DA).

41 An illustration of Boyden's philosophy: Lewis Perry, "Boyden of Deerfield" in The *Atlantic Monthly*, December 1942.

41 Ashley's journal and record of athletics: John P. and Thomas W. Ashley Papers, Alumni Files (DA).

42 Ashley outscored Flynt: "Monson is Loser" and "Tables are Turned" newspaper clippings in Ashley scrapbook (DA).

43 Flynt graduated from Monson Academy in 1912 and Williams College in 1916.

43 skunks: Miller; Ashley Papers (DA).

43 The Message of Our Flag: Typewritten copy of speech with FLB's instructions in margins is in T. W. Ashley Amherst Bio File (AC); John P. Ashley, *An Ashley Genealogy*, a paper read at the Pocumtuck Valley Memorial Association, 26 February 1924 (AC).

43 Hunting license: Thomas Williams Ashley Amherst Bio File (AC).

43 Football captain wrote: B. J. Connolly, Jr., to FLB, 24 September 1912 in T. W. Ashley Amherst Bio File (AC).

44 Schoolwork didn't come easy: T. Ashley to FLB, 2 November 1912 (DA).

44 Boyden arranges tutor: T. Ashley to FLB, 8 January 1913 (DA).

44 Coach predicts Tom as captain: Connolly to FLB, 24 September 1912 (AC).

44 31-0 rout: Ashley Genealogy (AC).

45 Tom coaches basketball: T. Ashley to FLB, 5 January 1916 (DA).

45 Tom seeks St. Marks job: Miller (DA).

45 Peter Bent Brigham Letter: undated FLB to T. Ashley, written on hospital stationery, discovered by Tina Cohen, Deerfield Academy Archivist, in FLB's 1934 appointment book (DA).

45 Tom proposes catalogue: T. Ashley to FLB, 28 July 1916 (DA); typescript of early catalogue draft (AC)

45 Tom enlists: undated clipping in Alumni File (DA); Sheldon quoted in Miller; F. L. Thompson, *Thomas Williams Ashley Eulogy* at Memorial Service, 1 September 1918 (AC).

47 Amherst senior thesis: T. Ashley Amherst Bio File (AC).

47 At Norfolk, VA: Ashley to FLB, 17 May 1917 (DA).

47 Charles Ashley afraid for Tom: C. H. Ashley to E. M. Whitcomb, 26 February 1918 in John Ashley Amherst Bio File (AC).

47 "Is Life Worth Living": T. Ashley Amherst Bio File (AC).

47 "A definite goal": T. Ashley to FLB, 6 February 1918 (DA).

47 Tom teaches soldiers: T. Ashley to FLB, 6 February 1918 (DA).

47 German Spring offensive: Robert B. Asprey, *At Belleau Wood*, 1965; and *Army and Navy Journal*, 17 August 1918 in T. Ashley Amherst Bio File (AC)

48 Keller Rockey: Rockey to C. H. Ashley, 2 November 1919 (AC).

48 The Germans attack: *Army and Navy Journal* (AC).

49 Lt. R.M. Wilcox: quoted in Ashley Genealogy (AC).

49 Cpl. Charles Murphy: Murphy to C. H. Ashley undated, T. Ashley Amherst Bio File (AC).

49 Cut down by a machine gun: report of Lieutenant L. Y. Stallings undated, T. Ashley Amherst Bio File (AC).

49 Disregards death: "Is Life Worth Living," T. Ashley Amherst Bio File (AC).

10. THE BOARDING DEPARTMENT

51 Playground Association offers FLB job: FLB "offered a position as field secretary at a great advance in salary," undated newspaper clipping (DA).

52 Gibbs persuades FLB to stay at DA: Gibbs to FLB, 25 August 1914 (DA). 53

53 Anti-Aid Amendment: The *New York Times*, 5 November 1917, 8 November 1917.

53 "You can be elected": Beard to Boyden, 27 February 1917 (DA).

54 "A strategy as well as an ideal": FLB Talks (DA).

54 "I was very green": McPhee Notes, Box III, 16 "Public Funds '24" (DA).

54 John McCormack: Hon. John McCormack to Hon. David N. Edlestein, 28 October 1959 (DA).

54 FLB's interest in Gibbs: Gibbs to FLB, 2 November 1914 (DA).
55 Gibb's placement service: brochure in FLB Friends (DA).
55 "sic me on": Gibbs to FLB, 25 May 1916 (DA).
55 FLB to Mrs. Breed: 31 August 1949 (DA).

11. A PREP SCHOOL

57 College preparatory, well-rounded education: *Deerfield Viewbook 1919* (DA).
58 Italian farmer letter: FLB Talks (DA).
58 Cost of dormitory: *Deerfield School Committee and DADHS Annual Reports 1919-1921* (DA).
58 FLB revered Perry: *Phillips Exeter Academy Bulletin*, January 1970 (DA).
59 Perry and hitchhikers: The *New York Times*, 28 January 1970.
59 Perry describes FLB's Exeter visit: The *Atlantic Monthly*, December 1942.
60 FLB quotes Robert E. Lee: FLB Talks (DA): McPhee, p. 18.
61 A Tennessee boy: FLB to W. T. Garrison, 22 November 1920 (DA).
61 A Jewish boy: George Rogers to FLB, 27 December 1921 (DA).
62 "Pumpkin pie as a missile": C. Wardell St. John to FLB, 4 March 1922 (DA).

12. SALESMANSHIP

63 "Elementary consideration and kindness": FLB Talks (DA).
63 FLB emphasizes courtesy: *Pocumtuck*, April 1921 (DA).
64 Shoes shined and a clean shirt: McPhee Notes (DA).
64 Litter: *Pocumtuck*, April 1921 (DA).
64 Athletics as advertising: *Pemawachuatuck*, June 1914 (DA).
64 FLB schedules Choate game: FLB to George St. John, 20 October 1921 (DA).
64 St. John impressed: George St. John to FLB, undated Spring 1922 (DA).
65 Deerfield defeats Loomis: FLB to R.W. Maynard, 16 January 1922 (DA).
65 DA boys prepare for Amherst: *Pocumtuck*, Thanksgiving 1921 (DA).
65 Barton biographical sketch: Stephen Fox, *The Mirror Makers*. 1984; Bruce Barton '07 Amherst College Bio File (AC).
66 FLB asks Barton for help: FLB to Barton, 30 November 1920 (DA).

13. OBSTACLES

69 Coleman editorial: undated clipping, *Greenfield Recorder and Gazette* in Public Funds File (DA).
69 A fox from Foxboro: Public Funds File (DA).
70 Elizabeth Pratt Whitman: undated clipping, *Greenfield Recorder and Gazette* in Public Funds File (DA).
71 Harriet Childs editorial: Public Funds File (DA).
71 Childs seeks job: Childs to FLB, 1 January 1914 (DA).

72 Plunkett's objection, a one man school: FLB to Frederick H. Payne, 21 February 1923 (DA).

72 Maynard seeks independent school: Maynard to FLB, 18 January 1922 (DA).

73 "without being conceited": FLB to Payne (DA).

73 "woefully inadequate" physical plant: FLB to Payne (DA).

74 "push that legal investigation": Maynard to FLB, 18 January 1922 (DA).

75 "reconciled to start something else": FLB to Maynard, 23 October 1922 (DA).

75 "until the last gun is fired": FLB to Maynard, 25 October 1922 (DA).

14. DEALMAKING

77 Meicklejohn and Coolidge endorsements: DA Promotional Flyer 1923 (DA); Coolidge to Maynard, 3 March 1923 (DA).

77 George Pratt's lead gift: FLB to Maynard, 5 January 1921 (DA).

78 Perry approaches Harkness: Lewis Perry to George Plimpton, 20 December 1922 (DA).

78 Harkness pledges $100,000: Harkness to Perry, 20 December 1922 (DA).

78 Stearns approaches Morrow: Al Stearns to Dwight Morrow, 29 November 1922 (DA).

79 Gibbs visited Boyden: Gibbs to Wilmot Trevoy, 30 November 1922 (DA).

80 "Make it WHAT IT SHOULD BE": *Pocumtuck*, Thanksgiving 1921 (DA).

80 "Sell the School": *Pocumtuck*, Spring 1921 (DA).

80 February Town Meeting: described in FLB to J.M.A. Sheldon, 12 March 1923 (DA).

81 Pro-Boyden handbill: 1923 Crisis File (DA).

82 FLB begged Stearns: FLB to Stearns, 27 March 1923 (DA).

82 Stearns wired the Pratt brothers: Stearns to Herbert, George, and John Pratt, and Dwight Morrow, 31 March 1923 (DA).

82 Cleeland, Maynard, Frank Stearns underwrite academy: FLB to Al Stearns, 12 April 1923 (DA).

82 Dickinson's explicit intention: Esther Dickinson, Last Will and Testament (DA).

83 *Springfield Union* reports Crosby's holding: "Deerfield Academy Suit Comes To Final Close" undated clipping in 1923 Crisis File (DA).

84 "A big and famous academy": FLB to William Davenport 1924 (DA).

15. BEGINNING AGAIN

86 Boys sleeping in pool room: FLB to C. T. Plunkett, 13 February 1924 (DA).

86 "We scrape in unison": *Pocumtuck*, 24 February 1924 (DA)

86 The staged gym picture: Maynard to FLB, 21 January 1924 and FLB to Maynard, 23 January 1924 (DA).

86 Plunkett pledged a dorm: Plunkett to FLB, 10 April 1925 (DA).

86 Barton knew little: Barton to G. B. Mallon, 29 March 1924 (DA).

87 Boyden's definition of New England conscience: FLB Talks (DA).
87 "Is this what you want?": Barton to E. S. Wilson, 3 March 1924 (DA).
88 Sheldon's interest in Girls Club: Sheldon to FLB, 31 August 1912 (DA).
88 "Good thorough Work!": Sheldon to FLB, 31 August 1912.
88 "Social center work is another thing": Sheldon to FLB, 31 August 1912 (DA)
88 Failure to hand write letters: Sheldon to FLB, 10 December 1922 (DA).
88 "absolute faith in each other": undated in Sheldon Trustee file (DA).
88 Sheldon co-signed: described in Maynard to FLB, 23 January 1922 (DA).
89 Simple and homespun: FLB Talks (DA).
89 "create a legend": Barton to FLB, 24 April 1924 (DA).
89 Sheldon pledges a science building: Sheldon to FLB, 24 October 1923 (DA).
90 Plunkett objects to FLB's unbusinesslike approach: Maynard to E. S. Wilson, 4 August 1925 (DA).
90 Sheldon abhorred Plunkett's handling of the school: Sheldon to FLB, 7 January 1926; Maynard to Wilson, 4 August 1925 (DA).
91 "more than onion growers": McPhee Notes, Box 3 Folder 16 (DA).
91 Moses persuaded Behrend and Coonley: Moses to FLB, 19 December 1927, 22 December 1927 (DA).
91 Wilson wrote Morrow: 23 June 1926 (DA).
91 Amherst alumni donated trophies: *Pocumtuck*, June 1924 (DA).
91 17 boys to Amherst: *Pocumtuck*, May 1925 (DA).
92 Merrill pledges $500: Merrill to FLB, 3 September 1926 (DA).
92 FLB and Merrill discuss scholarship: FLB to Merrill, 18 January 1927 (DA).
92 FLB's conflict with trustees: FLB to Maynard, 10 November 1926 (DA).
92 "Deerfield costs money!": McPhee, p. 80.
92 Not concerned with budgets: FLB to Maynard, 2 December 1927 (DA).
93 Someone else ought to direct: Maynard to FLB, 13 December 1927 (DA).
93 Plunkett's challenge gift: E. S. Wilson to Dwight Morrow, 12 July 1926 (DA).
93 Morrow's gift: Morrow to Wilson, 22 June 1926 (DA).
93 Deerfield broadens its support: Lewis Perry to FLB, 8 November 1928 (DA).
93 Harkness declines Wilson: Wilson to Morrow, 12 July 1926 (DA).
93 E. K. Hall as campaign chairman: Maynard to FLB, 10 November 1928 (DA).
94 "new modes of salesmanship and manufacture": *Scroll*, 18 February 1928 (DA).
94 "leaders in our national life": *Pocumtuck*, Thanksgiving 1926 (DA).

16. AMERICANIZATION

95 Principal of a Polish high school: FLB to J. Sheldon, 12 March 1923 (DA).
95 A public night school: P. F. Doyle to Myron Wilson, 10 February 1909, in *Deerfield School Committee Report 1909* (DA).
96 A crusade to Americanize the Poles: Trevoy to R. J. Cleeland, 3 July 1924, Deerfield Trustee File (DA).

96 "to help settle the Polish problem": FLB to Frederick Cooley, 28 March 1923 (DA).

97 A patriotic haven: FLB to E.T. Hartman, 2 May 1923 (DA).

97 FLB invites Appleton: FLB to W. S. Appleton, 12 November 1923; Appleton to FLB, 17 November 1923 (DA).

97 "preserve Deerfield": FLB to Appleton, 22 April 1924 (DA).

98 FLB approached Henry Ford: Maynard to FLB, 7 February 1925; FLB to Maynard, 2 May 1925 (DA).

98 Flynt meets FLB: *Greenfield Recorder and Gazette* clippings in Tom Ashley File (DA)

98 Flynt vowed not to collect: Donald R. Friary, "The Noncollectors: Henry and Helen Flynt" in *Antiques*, January 1982 (HD).

99 "sneaked out and saw the horses": Flynt to FLB, 22 November 1939 (DA).

99 Four homes for purchase: FLB to Maynard, 8 February 1938 (DA).

99 Flynt interested in preservation: Flynt to FLB, 7 October 1939 (DA).

99 Purchasing the Deerfield Inn: Flynt to FLB, 15 June 1939 (DA).

99 Flynt approaches Rockefeller: Flynt to FLB, 7 October 1939 (DA).

99 Flynt approaches Ford: Flynt to E. G. Liebold, Secretary to Henry Ford, 9 July 1941 (DA).

99 Land Acquisition Account: L. S. Heselton to FLB, 31 December 1941 (DA).

99 Flynt buys Manning property: Flynt to FLB, 31 December 1942 (DA).

100 "American standards must be maintained": FLB Talks (DA).

17. ELITISM

101 St. Grottlesex: refers to rival schools; St. Marks, St. Pauls, Groton and Middlesex.

101 FLB insisted against exclusion: Recreation Speech, 1913 (DA).

102 FLB wrote Elizabeth Greene: 3 February 1912 (DA).

102 A Jewish Latin Teacher: FLB to Dean Hanford, 8 December 1927 (DA).

103 "girls as day students": FLB to Porter Sargent, 14 January 1926 (DA).

103 "girls were always inferior specimens": Elizabeth Thorn Welford '20 to Lewis Perry, 18 February 1958 (DA).

103 Pink collar work: FLB to Elizabeth Thorn, 18 November 1920 (DA).

104 One day boy's mischief: FLB to Horace Moses, 25 June 1935 (DA).

104 Farmers burning crops: C. T. Crolius quoted in *Scroll* 1962 (DA).

105 Scholarships a financial burden: Maynard to FLB, 27 May 1933 (DA).

105 "big, strong, vigorous fellows": FLB to Sargent, 1 January 1922 (DA).

18. THE MIDAS TOUCH

107 "the greatest educational pickpocket": *Newsweek*, 19 February 1962.

107 "create a legend": Barton to FLB, 31 March 1934 (DA).

107 "be your best self": FLB quotes Samuel Goldwyn's "Why Everything Counts" in FLB Talks (DA).

107 Attention to social graces: *Scroll*, 1 March 1930 (DA).

108 New student indoctrination: Whitman B. Wells letter for 1962 *Scroll* (DA).

108 Positions Glee Club: FLB to Oatley, 14 April 1933 (DA).

109 The press as propaganda: FLB to Perry, 25 May 1962 (DA).

109 FLB quotes Socrates: *This Week Magazine*, 15 November 1963 (DA).

109 "more dough?": Barton to Matthew Brush, 15 November 1932 (DA).

109 deficit spending: FLB to Maynard, 19 January 1949 (DA).

110 Novak: *Scroll*, 2 February 1935, 27 February 1935 (DA).

110 Threadbare overcoat: oral interview with Vivien Peterson, 13 April 1990.

110 "I seem to be different": FLB remarks at New York Dinner, Headmaster's 50th Year Celebration (DA).

110 When Perry visited Deerfield: McPhee, p. 77.

111 "Does it have any furniture?": James W. Wickenden speech at The Headmasters Association Service of Remembrance for FLB, 9 February 1973 (DA).

111 Hockey Rink: oral interview with Doug Gortner, April 1990.

111 "Deerfield Academy was down and out": Perry to Malcolm Aldrich, 8 November 1959 (DA).

112 Sunday school story: FLB Talks (DA).

112 Boyden refused admission: McPhee Notes, Box III, File 15 (DA).

19. SPORTS

115 Amherst's semipro sluggers: *Amherst Student*, 22 February 1902, 22 March 1902, 12 May 1902 (AC).

115 Precepts of sportsmanship: *Amherst Student*, 15 March 1902 (AC).

116 Foxboro's sandlots: *Foxboro Reporter*, 2 August 1902, 16 August 1902, 6 September 1902.

116 A singles hitter: *Deerfield Alumni Journal*, Winter 1947 (DA).

117 "dumped into my own endzone": *Scroll*, 4 July 1955 (DA); Strauss, "Deerfield Headmaster is a Man of Action" in The *New York Times*, 2 November 1953.

117 NFL Hall of Fame: 14th Annual Awards Dinner, The National Football Foundation and Hall of Fame Program, 7 December 1971 (DA).

117 Reform college football: The *New York Times*, 10 October 1905, 12 October 1905, 15 October 1905, 19 October 1905, 10 November 1905, 27 November 1905, 28 November 1905, 29 November 1905, 5 December 1905, 8 December 1905, 10 December 1905, 29 December 1905.

117 E. K. Hall originates passing game: *Scroll*, 22 November 1932 (DA).

118 Sportsmanship Brotherhood: *Scroll*, 17 April 1954 (DA).

118 Teachers officate: Batchelder to FLB, 10 October 1930, 23 October 1930 (DA).

119 Memorable unbeaten season: *Greenfield Recorder*, 23 May 1945 (DA).

119 "support of The cheering section": *Pocumtuck*, April 1921 (DA).

119 Before the new fieldhouse: Grove quoted in *Scroll*, 6 October 1951 (DA).

120 Public schools seek uniforms: FLB to Ralph J. Walker, 6 October 1928 (DA).

120 Tall strapping boys: FLB to Horace Taft, 13 August 1921, Taft to FLB, 19 August 1921 (DA).

120 Bernie Redmond story: oral interview with Tim Engelland, April 1990.

121 Athletics and delinquency: FLB to Mr. Neale, 16 August 1955 (DA).

121 Marching at Choate: *Scroll*, 29 October 1939, 25 October 1952 (DA).

122 Sports build character: FLB Talks (DA).

122 Football story: FLB Talks (DA).

20. SINGING

123 Amherst singing: Fuess, pp. 350-51; *Amherst Quarterly*, May 1924, May 1926 (AC).

123 "the value of school songs": Dumont Lamb, 1904 Class History (DA).

123 Mary Eddy and Edwin Preble: letters written for 1962 *Scroll* (DA).

124 Objection to Oatley: F. A. Cook to FLB, 26 April 1922 (DA).

124 Oatley's ability: FLB to Oatley, 14 April 1933 (DA).

125 the first glee club: *Scroll*, 19 January 1935 (DA).

125 Romeo and Juliet: *Deerfield Alumni Journal*, Autumn 1945 (DA).

125 "Project you turkeys!": Lyman Brainerd '55 quoted in *Deerfield Alumni Journal*, July 1955 (DA).

125 Threatened to cancel a concert: FLB to Oatley, 14 April 1933 (DA).

126 1930 New York Sing: Maynard to FLB, 4 March 1930 (DA).

21. FACULTY

127 "running it for the boys": FLB remarks to faculty, opening school meeting 1966 (DA).

127 FLB quoted Pinchot: FLB Talks (DA).

128 Bob McGlynn story: McPhee, p. 65.

128 Daily Schedule: *Scroll*, 23 September 1959 (DA).

129 "persistent contact": FLB remarks, 1966 faculty meeting (DA).

129 "patience with minor failings": Wickenden speech, 1973 (DA).

129 "security and power of this school": 1966 faculty meeting (DA).

22. HORSES

131 "a lively horse to drive": *Newsweek*, 19 February 1962.

131 Loved horses as a youth: Sumner Kean, "A Man At The Reins" in The *Morgan Horse*, February 1953

131 Chaplain joke: FLB Talks (DA).
131 "Wizard of the Reins": *Poughkeepsie Sunday New Yorker*, 27 November 1955.
132 Murphy's friendship: FLB to Murphy, 7 May 1962 (DA).
132 Admiration for Murphy: FLB to Helen Meyer, 14 December 1955 (DA).
132 Horses and public relations: FLB remarks at New York Dinner 1952; FLB to Murphy, 11 March 1963 (DA).
133 "He didn't care about horses": oral interview with Bryce Lambert, May 1990.
133 "don't know anything about horses": FLB to Meyer, 14 December 1955 (DA).
133 Horses and boys: Hechinger, "The Boydens of Deerfield" in *This Week Magazine*, 15 November 1963.

23. FAMILY

135 "the same ways as at home": Hechinger.
135 "not much of a father": McPhee Notes, Box III, 3 (DA).
135 Mr. Micawber: McPhee, p. 35; McPhee Notes Box III, 19 (DA).
135 Brother Charles's proposition: Charles Boyden to FLB, 13 November 1921; FLB to Charles, 2 February 1922 (DA).
136 "I admire her": FLB Talks (DA).
136 "I don't know her really": McPhee Notes (DA).
136 "horse and buggy stage": FLB to Alice Cary, 23 July 1954 (DA).
136 Playing bridge: Randolph V. Miller to Helen Boyden, 10 January 1956, 50th Anniversary Scrapbook (DA).
137 Endicott Peabody: Frank Ashburn, *Peabody of Groton: A Portrait*, 1967. p. 129.
137 Sunapee retreat: McPhee Notes, Box III, 3 (DA).
137 A ride with Talisman: FLB to Murphy, 17 August 1948 (DA).
137 "the most selfish man": McPhee Notes, Box III, 3 (DA).
137 Betty Boyden: McPhee Notes (DA).
138 "helpmate": Hon. Silvio Conte, *Congressional Record*, 24 October 1973.

24. MRS. BOYDEN

139 Smith College Honorary Degree 1934.
139 Butterfield recalls: *Deerfield Alumni Journal*, Autumn 1944.
140 "the blue coated boy": Angell to H. Boyden, 12 June 1956 (DA).
140 Encouraged independent thinking: Sheldon to H. Boyden, 6 April 1931 (DA).
140 Romance of hydrogen and oxygen: *Deerfield Alumni Journal*, Autumn 1950.
140 Peter Atkinson recalls: *Scroll*, 20 April 1963 (DA).
141 Do the impossible: Tom Young to Helen Boyden, 9 April 1956 (DA).
141 Other fools: William V. Tripp III, *Scroll*, April 1963 (DA).
141 Memorable Boydenisms: *Scroll*, 10 May 1952, 9 June 1955 (DA).
141 Waldo Sessions recalls: *Scroll*, April 1963 (DA).

141 Steve Warck recalls: Warck to Helen Boyden, 28 December 1967 (DA).

142 By the headmaster's side: FLB to Terry Ferrer, 13 June 1957 (DA).

142 "far greater than my own": FLB to J. Wendell Setton, 13 June 1957 (DA).

143 Supporting Deerfield athletics: *Scroll*, 3 April 1959 (DA).

143 Male oases: McLachlan, p. 116-117.

143 "the finest woman I ever met": anonymous, *Dartmouth College Magazine*, 10 April 1953.

143 Marry a woman like Mrs. Boyden: Priscilla Abercrombie to H. Boyden (DA).

144 Mount Holyoke Honorary Degree 1961.

144 Together the Boydens created a great institution: *Greenfield Recorder*, 23 October 1973.

144 "stood in no man's shadow": Hon. Silvio Conte.

25. PUBLIC EDUCATION

145 A foolish argument: Hechinger.

145 Roosevelt wrote Boyden: FDR to FLB, 1 August 1935 (DA)

146 According to S. Burns Weston: S. Burns Weston, "Youth, Democracy, NYA and the Program Objective for Ohio," June 1940 in FLB NYA File (DA).

146 As an NYA advisor Boyden helped: Opening Remarks of Mr. Charles W. Taussig at Meeting of National Advisory Committee, 27 October 1941 (DA). Taussig to FDR: 28 October 1941 (DA). FLB to Taussig: 12 November 1941 (DA). FDR to Taussig: 14 July 1943 (DA). Taussig to FLB 21 July 1943 (DA).

146 Truman appoints Boyden: James F. Forrestal to FLB, 19 March 1946 (DA).

147 James J. McConaughy remarks: Statement to members of Navy Civilian Advisory Committee, 26 April 1946 (DA); Minutes of Navy Civilian Advisory Committee meeting, 26 April 1946, Doc. C-68517 (DA)

147 Air Group Four training maneuvers: Minutes of 26 April 1943 Meeting (DA) "Committee Goes to Sea to See How Navy Lives" The *New York Herald Tribune*, 2 June 1946. "Boyden Among 58 To Study Naval Career Advance" The *New York Herald Tribune*, 26 April 1946.

147 FLB to James F. Forrestal: 7 October 1948 (DA).

147 Naval Reserve: Bulletin of Information, Naval Reserve Officers Training Corps. and National Aviation College Program 1947 (DA).

148 Saltonstall appoints Boyden trustee: Harold Whiting Cary, *The University of Massachusetts: A Hundred Years*, 1962.

148 The University of Massachusetts's growth: Chris McGahan, "Let Us Now Praise Famous Men" in *Massachusetts Daily Collegian*, 31 January 1969 (UM).

148 "university at a fork in the road": Richard Glenn Gettell to FLB, 30 November 1959 (UM).

148 "nobody but a stupid man": Charles W. Cole to FLB 25 November 1959 (UM).

149 Boyden told a group: FLB notes for speech c. 24 November 1959 luncheon (DA).

149 Lederle considered the bill: President John W. Lederle Statement in *Massachusetts Daily Collegian*, 31 January 1969 (UM).

149 "An unparalleled achievement": *Massachusetts Daily Collegian*, 31 January 1969 (UM).

149 "no better or more consistent friend": "Headmaster Memorialized," *Boston Record American*, 10 May 1972.

26. LEADER

151 "one school men, one man schools": *Newsweek*, 3 June 1957.

151 "a towering figure": David N. Edelstein to Helen Boyden, 27 April 1972 (DA).

151 "kept within our abilities": Perry to FLB, 10 August 1961, FLB to Perry, 12 August 1961 (DA).

151 A perfect fit: Park, FLB Memorial Service 27 April 1972.

152 A favorite poem: "The Guy In The Glass" FLB Talks (DA).

152 "education and catastrophe": FLB Talks (DA).

152 Al Stearns: *The Challenge of Youth*, 1923.

152 "joy and fullness": Stephen Rockefeller '54, *Scroll*, 3 April 1952 (DA).

153 "Requisites of a Teacher": FLB Talks (DA).

154 "dream up something else": Merrill to FLB, 15 December 1951 (DA).

154 Tennyson's *Ulysses*: FLB's love for Tennyson dates to his Amherst years. He quoted this poem throughout his career and on numerous occasions in his final years.

BIBLIOGRAPHY

Ashburn, Frank. *Endicott Peabody: Peabody of Groton*, 1967.

Ashley, John P. *An Ashley Genealogy*, Pocumtuck Valley Memorial Association, 1924.

Asprey, Robert B. *At Belleau Wood*, G.P. Putnam, 1965.

Authelet, Jack. *Glimpses of Early Foxboro*, 1978.

Baltzell, E. Digby. *Philadelphia Gentlemen; The Making of a National Upper Class*, 1958.

———— *The Protestant Establishment*, 1964.

Barton, Bruce. *The Man Nobody Knows*, 1924.

Belasco, James A. *Teaching the Elephant to Dance: The Manager's Guide to Empowering Change*, Plume, 1991.

Bennis, Warren. *On Becoming A Leader*, Addison-Wesley, 1989.

———— *Why Leaders Can't Lead*, Jossey-Bass, 1990.

Bolman, Lee G. and Deal, Terrence E. *Reframing Organizations: Artistry, Choice, and Leadership*, Jossey-Bass, 1991.

Brautigan, Richard. *Trout Fishing In America*, Dell Publishing, 1967.

Churchill, Winston. *Coniston*, 1906.

Conger, Jay A. *The Charismatic Leader*, Jossey Bass, 1989.

Cooke, Brian P. "New England Academy Education in the Early Republic." in *Historical Journal of Massachusetts* (Winter 1993).

Cookson, Peter, and Persell, Carolyn. *Preparing for Power*, Basic Books, 1985.

Covey, Stephen R. *Principle-centered Leadership*, Summit Books, 1991.

Cremin, Lawrence. *History of American Education*, 1980.

Deerfield School Committee Reports 1901 to 1924.

DeForest, Charlotte Burgis. *An Undergraduate View of Smith College 1875-1908*.

Flynt, Henry N. "Notes of A Collector." in East Side House Winter Antiques Show *Catalogue* (1956).

————— "To Collect or Not To Collect: Notes About Old Deerfield and its Collections." (1963).

————— *Frontier of Freedom*, (1952).

Fox, Stephen. *The Mirror Makers: A History of Advertising and Its Creators*, 1984.

Foxboro Sesquicentennial Souvenir Booklet (1778-1928)

Friary, Donald R. "To Collect or Not To Collect: Helen and Henry Flynt at Historic Deerfield." (1972).

————— "The Noncollectors: Henry and Helen Flynt." *Antiques* (January 1982).

Frizzell, John Henry. "Frank L. Boyden Headmaster Extraordinaire." in *The Shield* of Phi Kappa Psi (Summer 1967).

Fuess, Claude Moore. *Amherst: The Story of A New England College*. Little, Brown, 1935.

Gardner, John W. *On Leadership.*, Free Press, 1990.

Hechinger. "The Boydens of Deerfield." in *This Week Magazine* (15 November 1963).

History and Directory of Foxboro (MA) 1890.

Howe, William S. "The Head's Spouse: From Super Mother to Tandem Biker." unpublished manuscript provided by Mr. Howe, Stanford University Graduate School of Education.

Kean, Sumner "A Man At The Reins." in *The Morgan Horse* (February 1953).

Kotter, John P. *Power and Influence*, Macmillan, 1985.

Kouzes, James M., and Posner, Barry Z. *Credibility: How Leaders Gain and Lose It, Why People Demand It*, Jossey Bass, 1994.

Krauschaar, Otto F. *American Nonpublic Schools*, 1972.

Lane, Clifford W., and Edith P. *This Was Foxborough!*, 1966.

Le Duc, Thomas. *Intellect and Piety at Amherst College*, 1969.

McLachlan, James. *American Boarding Schools*, 1970.

McPhee, John. *The Headmaster*, Farrar, Straus, Giroux, 1966.

————— Unpublished Notes and Materials for *The Headmaster*, Deerfield Academy Archives and Special Collections.

Miller, Amelia F. "Thomas Williams Ashley" in *Deerfield Alumni Journal* (Autumn 1962).

Mills, C. Wright. *The Power Elite*, 1956.

Perry, Lewis. "Boyden of Deerfield." in The *Atlantic Monthly* (December 1942).

Pfeffer, Jeffrey. *Managing With Power: Politics and Influence in Organizations*, Harvard Business School Press, 1992.

Plunkett, Charles T. Pamphlet Written *In Memoriam*, 13 October 1927, Berkshire Cotton Manufacturing Company.

Senge, Peter M. *The Fifth Discipline: The Art & Practice of The Learning Organization*, Doubleday, 1990.

Sheldon, George. *A History of Deerfield, Massachusetts*, 1972.

Sheldon, J. M. A. S. *Autobiographical Sketch*, unpublished manuscript available at Deerfield Academy Archives and Special Collections.

Spring, Joel. *The American School, 1642-1985*, 1986.

Stearns, Alfred E. *The Challenge of Youth*, 1923.

INDEX